20 AMICI
40 RICETTE

THE collective

BOOK STUDIO

Photographs by Nico Schinco

JOHN BERSANI

Friends and Food from the Heart of Chianti

20 AMICI
40 RICETTE

Library of Congress Cataloging-in-Publication Data available.

ISBN: 978-1-68555-668-6
Ebook ISBN: 978-1-68555-819-2
Library of Congress Control Number: 2024913263

Manufactured in China.

MIX
Paper | Supporting
responsible forestry
FSC® C102842

Printed using Forest Stewardship Council®certified
stock from sustainably managed forests.

Photographs by Nico Schinco.
Design by Rachel Lopez Metzger.

10 9 8 7 6 5 4 3 2 1

The Collective Book Studio®
Oakland, California
www.thecollectivebook.studio

*For my parents and grandparents — who showed me
the way.*

For my three children — who've shown me why.

And, of course, for Cyndy.

CONTENTS

INTRODUCTION

I can still vividly recall that hot, bright sunny morning. We'd arrived at Florence's Aeroporto Amerigo Vespucci—all six of us—bleary-eyed, jet-lagged, and more than a bit anxious. It was September 2001.

Less than a week earlier, I'd been sitting in our family room in Boston's western suburbs unable to do anything but numbly watch the 24/7 television coverage of the unimaginable events that had unfolded in Lower Manhattan. The images haunted me.

Now, on a tightly twisting road rising up toward a cypress tree–lined driveway on the outskirts of Florence, I found myself distracted by the prospect of maneuvering the eight-passenger van I'd just rented past an oncoming school bus. The road was narrow—at least by Stateside standards—and here were two unusually large vehicles—by Italian standards—jockeying for position in a game of chicken. There was no wiggle room. Both sides of the road were bordered by ancient stone walls. And there was no retreat. The road behind me dropped back down precipitously toward a blind curve.

As the bus approached, the driver laid on the horn. Only then did I notice a nun at the wheel in full-on traditional garb. I was about to start my four-month sabbatical in Italy in a traffic collision with a parochial school bus.

And then suddenly and unexpectedly—as would happen on so many future occasions during our time here—everything was okay. The driver-side rearview mirror grazed the school bus, snapped back into position, and we were both on our way without a scratch. The nun waved nonchalantly as she continued down the road.

Italy has a way of doing this to you. It'll throw you a curve when you least expect it only to leave you with a smile on your face, a story to tell, and another take on life in this beautiful, crazy, and at times frustrating place.

Fast-forward to today. My wife, Cyndy, and I live in a small town in the heart of the Chianti Classico wine appellation. We came for the food, the wine, the culture, and the natural beauty. We've stayed because of the people.

This book is a tribute to those people—our friends, our acquaintances, and the locals who make the heart of this place beat, day in and day out. It's a love letter to our town in all of its beautiful, quirky ways.

If you've purchased this book, it's most likely because you love to cook. And maybe you have your own love affair with Italy. I'd wager you're anxious to learn more about both. I hope the pages that follow will lead you to find your own path to great Italian cooking. Just as the people I profile bring their own spin to each and every dish here, this book should open your mind to putting your own imprint on every dish that comes out of your kitchen. It's the Tuscan way.

GAIOLE-IN-CHIANTI

This is a book about cooking. But it's also a book about people.

Like most expats and part-time residents from other parts of the world, it was Italy's seductive charms—its food, its wine, its rich history of art, architecture, and culture, its endless natural beauty—that drew us in. Our first few years living in Gaiole-in-Chianti, a small town just an hour south of Florence, year-round population just 2,750 souls, seemed like an extended vacation. But slowly, steadily, and almost imperceptibly, we morphed from seasonal vacationers who happened to own a home here to rooted locals with a network of friends who have kept us here.

Our Gaiolesi friends and neighbors have family histories and traditions that trace back several generations in this area that runs on wine production, agriculture, and, since the 1980s, tourism. The Chianti Classico wine appellation includes three historic wine-producing towns that formed the original "Lega del Chianti": Gaiole-in-Chianti, Radda-in-Chianti, and Castellina-in-Chianti. Gaiole may not be the prettiest or most picturesque of the three—just ask someone from Radda or Castellina—but in my opinion it is the most unspoiled and authentic and is less marred than its neighbors by everything that follows intense tourism.

In our American imaginations, Italy remains a country untouched by fast food, chain stores, and shopping malls. But that's not entirely true. Starbucks made its debut in Milan a few years back; McDonald's can be found in most large cities; prestige fashion brands like Prada, Gucci, and Ferragamo anchor large shopping malls on the outskirts of tourist destination cities; and supermarket chains like COOP have learned well

from their United States counterparts. Young Italians today live a very different life than their parents and grandparents.

That said, Italy is still a bastion of small family-run businesses, shops, and artisanal products. Especially in Italy's small towns. And Gaiole is a living example.

Our small town is fortunate to boast a historic and award-winning artisanal butcher shop; a bakery; a greengrocer selling seasonal fruits and vegetables; a family-run alimentare (basically a small specialty grocery store selling dried and canned goods, household products, fresh deli meats, cheeses, and prepared foods); and a well-curated enoteca offering a wide selection of the area's best wines. The simple pleasure of daily provisioning—and the personal rapport that develops with these dedicated shopkeepers—is a deeply satisfying part of life here.

A typical day starts at the Bar Centrale, where strong espresso, local gossip, political debate, and soccer banter make for a classic Italian experience. The owners are two brothers, Stefano and Giampaolo, who carry on in the footsteps of their father as they efficiently pull coffee after coffee, cappuccino after cappuccino. There are no crazy Starbucks combinations, no need to give your name, and—even when the line looks long—almost never a wait.

The morning coffee ritual is followed by a well-planned food shopping run. This is not one-stop supermarket shopping. This is multiple-stop personalized provisioning with advice and counsel—sometimes unsolicited—about what's best today and how you should prepare it. You might start out with the preconceived notion that you'll be making roast chicken for dinner only to pack up the car

with everything needed to prepare a slow braise of Chianina beef shoulder. It's what keeps things interesting and why you should embrace the Tuscan flair for kitchen improvisation.

You may not live in a small Tuscan hill town with food shopping opportunities like ours. But that doesn't mean you can't adopt and adapt. Adopt the Tuscan philosophy of seeking out the best ingredients from small shop owners you come to know and trust, and adapt your cooking as needed when you can't source some of the items called for in this book's recipes.

Back home in the U.S., there is growing demand for meat with a known provenance. When consumers buy a steak, they want to know who raised the steer, where it grazed, and what its diet was like. Yes, there's the save-the-world sustainability advocates who preach this type of consumer awareness. Me, I'm after flavor. Meat that is produced in this manner tastes better, period. Find a local butcher who is sourcing great meat products and develop a relationship with him or her. If you live somewhere that doesn't have a great butcher shop, consider one of the many first-rate online sources that are out there. You will pay a bit more, but the trade-off in taste and enjoyment will be worth it.

Think the same way about your fruits, vegetables, cheeses, and pantry items. Farmers' markets have proliferated in recent years all over the U.S. Find a cheese monger who can guide you to quality products. And specialty food shops and online purveyors offer everything from salt, capers, flour, and pasta to canned tomatoes, all carefully sourced from around the world.

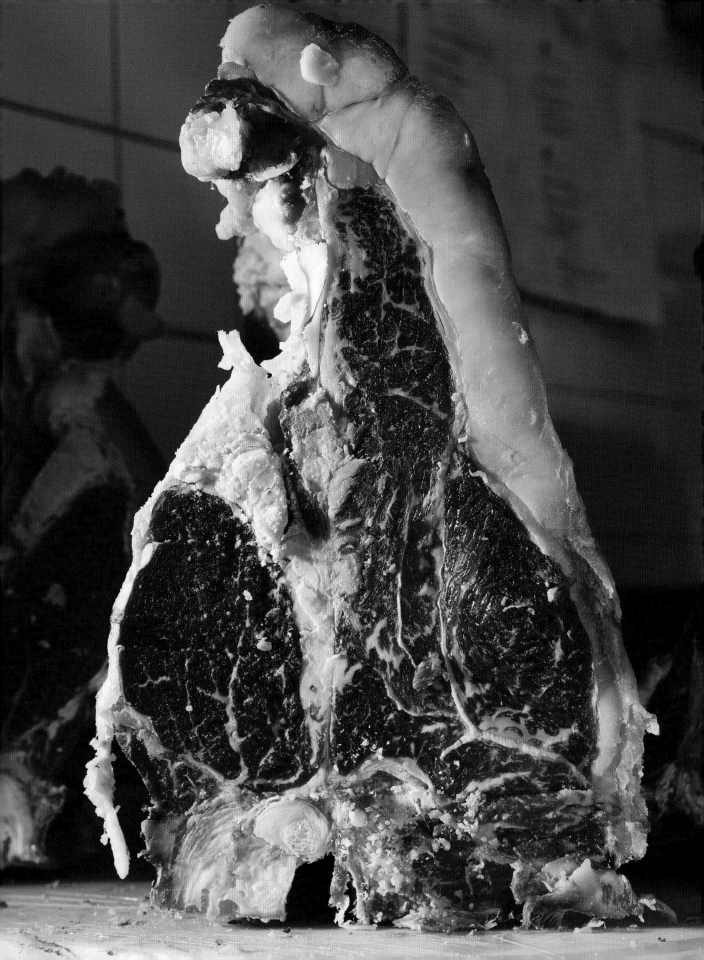

STORICA MACELLERIA
CHINI
1682

• CINTA SENESE •

• ALLEVAMENTO SEMIBRADO •

• PRODUZIONE ARTIGIANALE •

• SALUMI PREMIATI •

FRUTTA E VERDURA

THE PRELIMINARIES

Before we dive in, let's talk philosophy and pantry.

COOKING PHILOSOPHY

This book is full of recipes. And that worries me. Why, you ask? Isn't that the whole point of a cookbook?

First off, I don't think of this as strictly a cookbook. I hope the stories and profiles I've included engage you and transport you for a few minutes to another place.

But more importantly, I think cookbooks should be viewed and used as guides, not as a collection of strict formulas. Cooking is an art, not a science.

A recipe is really nothing more than the outline of an idea. It's a starting point. It can gently push you in the right direction with cues about what works and what doesn't. It's not meant to be rigid. It should encourage you to explore your own way forward. It should set you free, not tie you down.

As beginning cooks, we all lean heavily on recipes. We're not yet completely familiar with basic cooking techniques. We're not yet confident in our judgment of quantities. We don't yet trust ourselves to instinctively know when a steak is perfectly cooked or when our pasta has reached that elusive texture we call al dente.

It's okay to lean on recipes as you're learning. That's why cookbooks serve as an important learning—and confidence-building—tool. But with time and experience, you'll find yourself less reliant on recipes and more reliant on your own cooking instincts. And that's when things start to be fun.

The friends that I introduce in this book are all great home cooks—some are professionals. They all have their own culinary signature. They create food from memories and vision, not from recipes. Their recipes—some appearing in a book for the first time—serve only as a way to communicate what they instinctively know. They allow you to develop your own feel for a dish.

Have fun with this book. Don't sweat or stress over the details. If your first attempt at a dish doesn't turn out the way you'd hoped, take note of where you think you went wrong and try to correct things on the next try. Or, maybe you liked the result, but know you could improve it even more with the addition of an herb that you really like or the deletion of an ingredient that you don't.

Another very Tuscan cooking philosophy: "Non si butta niente!"—Nothing gets thrown out!

Here in the U.S. we are fortunate to live in the land of plenty. We go to the grocery store and take for granted the vast bounty of choices offered. The modern supermarket really is a marvel of food production technology, transportation logistics, and business ingenuity. We can sometimes find fault with the system—the food writer Michael Pollan has made a career of it. But at the same time, I think we must acknowledge that our food supply and distribution system is a modern miracle. And we should honor every ingredient available by minimizing waste. It's not just the right thing to do, but it can also make for some really delicious food.

A roast chicken leaves a carcass; that carcass can give its best to a homemade chicken stock. Any leftover meat can be finely minced, mixed with reconstituted stale bread, some cheese grated from a nearly finished rind, some herbs on their last leg in the fridge, an egg, and bingo! You've got some delicious chicken meatballs for another evening's dinner. That homemade stock goes into a risotto; the leftover risotto becomes the base for tomorrow evening's arancini appetizer. And so it goes . . .

Throughout this book, I'll offer ideas for

extending ingredients and using leftovers to create new dishes. And together, we'll try to extract flavor from what we might otherwise discard as scraps and waste. You'll never look inside your fridge the same way again.

THE TUSCAN PANTRY

Italian cooking, and regional Tuscan cooking in particular, is deceptively simple. Most dishes involve no more than three or four primary ingredients. Once you surpass five, a Tuscan will begin to look at you with dripping skepticism.

With few ingredients in play, there is no room for compromise in quality. Second-rate products will have nowhere to hide. Find the best-quality ingredients you can and pay the premium required. The payoff—better taste, nutrition, and satisfaction—will be worth the additional cost.

A well-stocked Tuscan pantry contains certain staples that form the backbone of its cuisine. With these key ingredients at hand, a spur-of-the-moment dinner can come together in no time. All you need is some imagination, a touch of inspiration, and a few basic kitchen skills.

Here are the key pantry items that I can't do without.

OLIVE OIL

High-quality extra-virgin olive oil is the foundation of great Italian cooking. With the exception of Italy's northernmost regions—where olive trees are unable to thrive and butter comes into play—each regional cuisine depends heavily upon the flavor profile and flavor-enhancing qualities of great oil.

What makes a great oil? First off, great fruit. Many experts prefer monovarietal (sometimes called monocultivar) oils—those produced from one single type of olive. But many great oils are produced from blends. In Chianti, for example, it's not uncommon for a high-quality oil to be

made from blending as many as five to seven different types of olives. Second, and perhaps most important, the best oils are produced from early harvest olives. These are olives that are still mostly green and produce spicy, peppery, and slightly bitter oil. These early harvest oils are the best flavor enhancers, although they sometimes can be difficult to find.

Another consideration: freshness. From the moment it's pressed onward, olive oil begins to gradually deteriorate as it's exposed to oxygen, light, and heat. Within a year or so, the best qualities of an oil have dissipated. Within two years, the oil may be rancid or close to it.

Unfortunately, most olive oil commercially sold in the U.S. is well past its prime. Check the label carefully before purchasing. If there is no bottling or harvest date indicated or if the date is more than a year past, don't buy the oil.

Many oils are also misleadingly labeled. For example, just because an oil carries an Italian name or even if the label indicates that it is a product of Italy, that doesn't necessarily mean it's an authentic Italian olive oil. The olives may have been purchased from a source in another country—at a cheaper price—and then pressed and bottled in Italy. Or the oil itself might have been purchased elsewhere by the bottler and simply packaged at an Italian facility. You want an oil whose label indicates that it was produced with olives grown by an Italian producer, preferably on the producer's estate, and pressed and bottled at or near the estate. In other words, provenance matters.

Find a trusted source and invest in great oil. Don't be timid about using your best-quality oil. Many "authorities" recommend using high-quality oil only for finishing dishes or for dressing salads. They advise that a lower-quality oil is an acceptable substitute for cooking and frying. Don't

believe it. There is no substitute for high-quality olive oil in great Italian cooking. Will using high-quality oil with reckless abandon cost you more? Yes. But if you're reading this, then you care about what you cook and what you eat. That marginal investment is something you're going to be happy about.

SALT

I have a large collection of cookbooks acquired over many years. One of my favorites—and one I always recommend to friends looking to up their game in the kitchen—is *Ruhlman's Twenty*, by the prolific food writer Michael Ruhlman. It won a James Beard award.

Ruhlman lists and elaborates on what are, in his opinion, the twenty most important techniques in great cooking. You'll find many that you'd expect, such as "Roast," "Braise," and "Sauté." Others are less obvious. The first chapter is titled "Think." Others include "Onion" and "Water."

Technique number two is "Salt." I'd never thought of salt as a cooking technique, but Ruhlman forever changed my perspective on this most important of all cooking ingredients.

Salt is the single most important and effective flavor enhancer in a cook's arsenal. As the late, great Italian cooking instructor and author Marcella Hazan once said: "Salt is a magnet. It draws flavor from food."

In today's health-conscious world, many view salt as something harmful—something to be avoided. Certainly for those who suffer from hypertension, too much salt intake can be a bad thing. But as with most everything in life, moderation and common sense should guide us. Without salt, our food would be seriously lacking in taste and complexity. Nine times out of ten, if I taste a dish in progress and something seems off, it needs more salt.

As with all ingredients, when we talk salt, there's the high-quality, artisanally produced version and the mass-produced industrial alternative. Seek out the former. It will make a huge difference in how your food tastes.

Naturally produced salts without chemical additives or preservatives are what you want. Many great salts are produced throughout the world. Among Italian salts, it's tough to beat those from the salt flats of Trapani, Sicily.

Keep in mind that different salts have different flavor profiles and, most importantly, different flavor intensities. Depending on a given salt's coarseness and salinity, a teaspoon of one may be much stronger than a teaspoon of another. Remember, recipes and recipe quantities are guides, not scientific doctrine. Taste as you go along and use your palate and personal judgment to determine how much salt is the right amount.

For everyday use, I like the flavor profile, moderate intensity, and texture of the simple kosher salt produced by Diamond Crystal. I also stock our pantry with coarse seat salt from Trapani. Coarse sea salt could be your everyday all-purpose choice and will also serve as a great finishing salt.

CANNED TOMATOES AND TOMATO PASTE

Let's face it, although regional Italian cooking is based on a lot more than tomato sauce, we Americans are prone to think first of exactly that. And we're not entirely wrong. Quality canned tomatoes play an important role in most regional Italian cuisines. And the king of all canned tomatoes is the San Marzano.

Let's be clear. When we talk about San Marzano tomatoes, we need to understand that it's not just the tomato variety that's important, but it's also where the tomato is grown. San Marzanos are a variety of plum tomato, especially sweet with

grown (not just canned) in Italy from the region of Campania. Look for the DOP certification of provenance. Even some Italian purveyors play tricks with the labeling: "Product of Italy" does not necessarily (and usually doesn't) mean "Made in Italy" or "Grown in Italy." Such corner-cutting purveyors are buying tomatoes from foreign sources (many from China!) and passing them off as the real deal at too-good-to-be-true (because it isn't true) low prices. Don't be fooled.

High-quality tomato paste should also have a place in your pantry. It's readily available from specialty food retailers and, in jarred or tubed format, can be stored for up to six months in your refrigerator after being opened. A small amount, when added judiciously to pasta sauces, soups, or braising meats, brings an added depth of flavor to finished dishes. Artisanal tomato concentrate from Sicily—where the natural drying and preserving process is an honored tradition—is my preferred choice.

DOPPIO ZERO "00" FLOUR

Fresh pasta is the skilled combination of eggs, flour, and maybe a few other wet ingredients. Most of the time, the flour in play is farina doppio "00"— double zero flour. The double zero designation refers to the fineness, not the strength or protein content, of the flour. Double zero is the finest-grade milled flour with an almost powdery consistency. It produces fresh pasta that's silky with a melt-in-the-mouth texture.

If you plan to invest time in learning the art of making fresh pasta, then farina doppio "00" should have a place in your pantry. Though you can achieve acceptable results with all-purpose flour, you'll find a noticeable difference when you use double zero. A good brand that's readily available in specialty food shops in the U.S. is Antimo Caputo. It's also the preferred brand of Italian pizza makers.

a balanced acidity that is particularly good for cooked sauces. Is it possible to grow San Marzanos in California? Yes. Will they be the best you can find? In my experience, definitely not.

The best San Marzanos are grown in Italy in the region of Campania (think Naples and surrounding areas), where a unique combination of microclimate and soil produces prized tomatoes that have earned DOP (denominazione di origine protetta) status. And the best of the best are grown within a particular appellation/subzone known as the Agro Nocerino Sarnese in the province of Salerno. My favorite producer is DaniCoop, whose Gustarosso-labeled DOP San Marzanos are among the best I've ever tasted. They're a bit more expensive than some competitors, but worth every cent.

Again, buyer beware: provenance matters. Check the label on canned tomatoes. Make sure that you're getting San Marzano variety tomatoes

DRIED PASTA

Speaking of pasta, let's make an important distinction. There are two types of pasta: dried and fresh. Fresh pasta is made for the most part with flour and eggs, with the possible addition of a little olive oil and/or water. These are the silky-smooth noodles—fettucine, tagliatelle, pappardelle, lasagna, and stuffed pasta shapes, such as ravioli, agnolotti, and tortelloni—that star in dishes like tagliatelle alla bolognese, pappardelle al cinghiale, lasagna, and tortellini in brodo.

Then there's dried pasta. Dried pastas are produced with water and hard durum and/or semolina flour. The resulting dough is mechanically pressed through dies to form shapes such as spaghetti, linguine, penne, rigatoni, and paccheri, to name just a few. The pasta is dried and sold in packages with a long shelf life.

Typically, fresh pastas are handmade on an as-needed basis in restaurant kitchens and homes throughout Italy. Dried pasta is left to artisans who operate pasta factories—some being small-batch artisanal producers while others (think Barilla) operate on a huge industrial scale.

Some of the best dried pastas come from an area in the Campania region known as Gragnano. These are DOP status pasta products. The best of the best use bronze dies for the extraction of the pasta shapes, producing a rough pasta surface perfect for holding sauces. These high-quality producers also dry their pasta slowly and at low temperatures, ensuring a final product that holds its integrity during cooking.

You'll spend a bit more for quality dried pastas, but, once again, the taste return on investment will be well worth it.

BEANS

Tuscans love beans. All kinds of beans. Three of the most popular and widely used varieties are zolfini, cannellini, and borlotti. While not always interchangeable, all three appear in many of Tuscan cuisine's classic bean-based dishes, such as ribollita, zuppa di fagioli, and fagioli all'uccelletto.

Search out good-quality dried beans. They have a long shelf life and can be easily stored in a cool, dry place. Canned or jarred beans can also be very good and are certainly more convenient when you're pressed for time, as they do not require any presoaking. In my experience, quality beans packed in their own cooking water are the best to work with as a substitute for dried beans.

CHEESE

No question: "local" is second nature in regional Italian cooking—something that is practiced without the preaching; something implicit on restaurant menus without four extra lines of text and a footnote.

Consistent with that philosophy, you will find pecorino toscano, an aged sheep's milk cheese produced in various parts of the Tuscan countryside, playing a leading role in many dishes. It's delicious eaten on its own or grated over pasta and soups. Sharp, pungent, and salty, it adds an unmistakable depth of flavor to food. In the U.S., I find it somewhat difficult to source high-quality pecorino cheese from Tuscany at a reasonable cost, but better cheese purveyors do carry it. Make it part of your pantry arsenal.

Even Tuscans, as provincial and biased as they can be in preferring everything Tuscan over anything else, make exceptions for exceptional products. And there is no denying that Parmigiano-Reggiano cheese is an exceptional product.

Parmigiano-Reggiano has been called the "King of Cheeses." It's certainly one of the world's most loved and most widely consumed—and widely counterfeited. This classic cheese should have a place in any respectable Italian pantry.

Produced in Italy's Emilia-Romagna region, this umami bomb is made from 100 percent cow's milk in accordance with strict DOP rules, guidelines, and traditions. It's great eaten on its own—maybe with a drop of beautiful aged balsamic vinegar. But this cheese is the gold standard grated on pasta, soups, and risotto. And any number of roasted vegetables can be finished with a sprinkling and then browned one last time in a hot oven to add another layer of flavor.

Look to a trusted source for your Parmigiano-Reggiano—a local cheese monger, preferably—and note the distinct DOP mark of the cheese consortium on the rind of the big wheel. That's the sign of authenticity.

Parmigiano-Reggiano must be aged in accordance with DOP rules for a minimum of twelve months. Some producers age for longer periods—twenty-four months, thirty-six months, and even longer. The best way to determine what you prefer is to taste. In general, cheeses aged in the twelve- to twenty-four-month range are best suited to grating, while older wheels are ideal for straight-up cheese eating.

FRESH HERBS

If you walk along small roads in the Tuscan countryside, the smell of wild herbs and flowers is everywhere. Farmhouses are surrounded by rosemary hedges, sage, and lavender. If you know where to look, you can find the indigenous herb known as "nepitella." I'd describe it as a wild relative of thyme.

Fresh herbs play an important role in Tuscan cooking. Try your hand at planting your own rosemary bush, a patch of thyme, some sage, and maybe some oregano. It's great to walk out your

door and gather what you need as you cook. But if time or climate doesn't allow for your own personal herb garden, no worries. Fresh herbs are widely available today on supermarket shelves, and stored properly in your refrigerator, they can last for up to a week.

CHILE PEPPER

Sometimes you need to bring the heat. Although Tuscan regional cooking is not particularly known for its spiciness, chile pepper is often used—with a restrained hand—to add a hint of teasing heat to pasta sauces or complexity to certain vegetable preparations. Our pantry is always provisioned with fresh, dried, and preserved chile peppers, each of which plays a role in certain dishes.

Fresh chile peppers come in a dizzying array of colors, shapes, sizes, and heat intensities. The only way to know for sure what to use—and what you prefer—is to carefully taste them. For more powerful varieties, it's sometimes best to use a whole, uncut pepper and remove it after cooking. For peppers with a more moderate flavor profile, a quick mincing will best release their heat. A bit of trial and error may be required to find the right level of heat for you.

Dried chile peppers are also very common in regional Italian cooking. We've all seen crushed red pepper flakes on grocery store shelves. But the preferred alternative is whole dried chiles, which may come on a vine, or may be bagged or jarred. Whole dried chiles will retain their heat "kick" for much longer than their pre-crushed cousins, which tend to fade rapidly in taste. Again, as with fresh chile peppers, the heat intensity of dried chile peppers will vary from one type to another.

Finally, there are preserved chile peppers. These are fresh peppers that usually have been chopped and then preserved in oil. The chile peppers themselves, as well as the oil they have been preserved in, are great heat-inducing condiments. The gold standard—in my personal opinion—are preserved Calabrian chile peppers, available in better supermarkets and from specialty food retailers. The Divina brand is imported to and readily available in the U.S., has an excellent spicy/sweet balance of flavor and will keep almost indefinitely in your refrigerator.

* * *

So . . . you've heard a bit about our story. I've introduced you to our small village here in the heart of Chianti. I've shared some thoughts about my cooking philosophy and how I hope this book might up your personal kitchen game. And we've talked about what should be in your pantry and the importance of product provenance. Now it's time to meet some friends and cook some delicious food.

HOW TO USE THIS BOOK

Before we start, I'd like to offer a few ideas on how to get the most from this book. First and foremost, please do cook from it. This is a book that is meant to be used. Yes, it's filled with beautiful images and what I hope are interesting background stories. But I'd be disappointed if a reader relegated it solely to coffee table or nightstand status. This is a book that should have a place in your kitchen. The recipes that follow are approachable and within the technical reach of even kitchen newbies. Please cook from this book!

The way this book is organized—by friend rather than by category of dish—is nontraditional. Rather than grouping together all antipasti, all pastas and soups, all main courses, and all side dishes in dedicated chapters, I'm taking you on a culinary journey through the eyes of friends who love to cook. Consequently, any given chapter may or may not include all the components of a complete lunch or dinner. To compensate, where and when appropriate, I'll make suggestions about how a particular dish might be combined with another or what role a dish typically plays within the context of an authentic Tuscan meal. Better yet, you should feel free to combine the dishes that appeal to you in any way that fits your personal preferences and the tastes of your family and friends.

Now let's get cooking . . .

LUCIANO

In the United States, a lot of men become obsessed with golf. In Tuscany, many become obsessed with mushrooms. My friend Luciano is one of those mushroom fanatics. Luciano enjoys nothing more than rising at four thirty in the morning and heading to one of his well-kept secret foraging spots deep in the Tuscan forest. If you know where to look and if weather conditions are just right—usually during the wetter spring and fall months—you'll find the prized porcini mushroom.

Passionate mushroom foragers throughout Italy take their hobby very seriously and guard their secrets closely. There's a friendly competition in small hill towns throughout Chianti. Every mushroom hunter worth his weight in dried porcini is certain that he will find the most and the biggest.

Me? I just like to eat them, whether grilled over an open fire, sliced raw and dressed with good olive oil and lemon juice, or, best of all, tossed with handmade tagliatelle. Here's how Luciano does it.

TAGLIATELLE AI FUNGHI PORCINI
Tagliatelle with Porcini Mushrooms

Early spring in Chianti can be cruel. It'll tease you with a string of warm, sunny weather, then rain for days on end. There is a silver lining: fresh porcini. Porcini-based dishes can be found on trattoria menus throughout the year. But the mushrooms have either been frozen (something that by law must be noted on menus) or imported from other parts of Europe. Spring rains bring fresh, locally foraged porcini to restaurant tables—in salads, in omelets, and, of course, in this iconic Tuscan pasta classic.

Note: If you don't have the time or inclination to prepare the fresh pasta, there are many high-quality fresh and dried pasta noodles available in better supermarkets and specialty food shops.

SERVES 4

Kosher or coarse sea salt

1 garlic clove

¼ cup (60 ml) best-quality extra-virgin olive oil, plus more as needed

8 ounces (225 g) fresh porcini mushrooms (or substitute cremini or portobello), cut into bite-size pieces

1 small dried chile pepper, crushed (optional)

1 sprig fresh thyme

Freshly ground black pepper

1 pound (475 g) fresh pasta sheets (page 58), cut into long noodles using a pasta machine attachment or by hand

1. Bring a large pot of water to a rolling boil over high heat; salt the water generously.

2. Place the flat side of a kitchen knife on top of the garlic clove and come down on it with your hand, using enough force to flatten the clove and loosen the skin. Remove the skin from the garlic clove and place it in a large sauté or frying pan with the olive oil. Over medium-low heat, bring the olive oil and garlic to a slow, steady sizzle. You don't want to burn the garlic, just achieve a nice yellow color.

3. Add the mushrooms, crushed chile pepper (if using), and thyme to the pan. Season with salt and pepper and stir with a wooden spoon to incorporate everything together. Cook the mushrooms over medium heat for 5 to 7 minutes. Initially, the mushrooms will soak up the oil, brown, and release the liquid within them. After a bit more time, they will begin to release the oil they previously soaked up. At that point, taste for seasoning and, if needed, add more salt or pepper.

4. Put the pasta into the boiling salted water and cook until al dente for dried pasta or until "punto giusto" for fresh pasta (see Some Thoughts on Pasta, page 36).

5. As the pasta is cooking, place the mushroom mixture over medium heat and add a large spoonful of the pasta cooking water to the pan. Mix with your wooden spoon and let the mixture cook down into a saucy consistency. If it becomes too dry, add another spoonful of the cooking water. The goal here is to emulsify the mushroom mixture with the pasta water to create a sauce that's not too watery and not too dry.

—continued—

TAGLIATELLE AI FUNGHI PORCINI
(continued)

To finish the dish

6. When the pasta is cooked to the correct point, use a pair of kitchen tongs to drain and remove it from the pot, and toss it directly into the pan with the mushroom mixture.

7. You are now at a critical point in pasta cooking. It's time to "marry" your sauce with the pasta. Over medium-low heat, stir the pasta into the mushroom mixture thoroughly, coating all of the noodles with the sauce. If the combination of pasta and mushrooms seems too dry, which is likely at this point as the pasta absorbs some of the sauce you created, add some more pasta cooking water until you achieve a balanced emulsification.

8. Remove the pan from the heat. Add a drizzle of olive oil to the pan and mix one last time to incorporate. Portion the pasta into warmed bowls and serve immediately. A mushroom fanatic like Luciano would frown at the thought of adding cheese to this dish (he'd claim it masks the beautiful flavor of the porcini), but you should follow your heart.

Make It a Meal: These tagliatelle stand well on their own as a main course with a simple antipasto of bruschette miste (page 173), or serve half portions as a starter course or "primo" in the Italian tradition.

Wine Pairing: Rocca di Montegrossi Chianti Classico DOCG 2020. The balanced fruit and earthiness of this wine from Gaiole's Monti subzone is the perfect accompaniment to any mushroom-centric dish.

SOME THOUGHTS ON PASTA

A bowl of pasta . . . it seems so simple. Boil some water; dump in your pasta; cook, drain, and add it to your sauce; dinner on the table. But if that's your approach, you will be shortchanging yourself and your guests. There are some techniques, nuances, and details that can take your pasta cookery from acceptable to extraordinary.

I hate to say this, because it's the expected mantra of the smug Italophile, but most of the pasta we are served in the U.S. is not very good. There are, of course, exceptions. There are well-known American chefs who have served apprenticeships in Italy and have brought back the passion, traditions, and techniques that make eating pasta in Italy such a great sensory experience. But you have to search far, and you have to open your wallet wide.

Throughout Italy, great pasta is ubiquitous. It's everywhere. And for Italian cooks—professionals and home cooks alike—it's almost second nature. Sure, you might be served something substandard at a tourist trap. And you might overpay for a Michelin-star pasta experience. But in local trattorias throughout Italy, beautiful pasta dishes at incredibly affordable prices are the norm.

SOME PASTA TIPS:

Best Quality Only. Use only high-quality dried or fresh pasta. For dried pastas, protein content should be at least 13 percent. Anything less and your pasta will break apart during cooking.

Don't Overcrowd. Use a pot plenty large enough to accommodate lots of water; you do not want to overcrowd your pasta.

Season Properly. Season your pasta water generously with salt. How much is enough? Taste it. The pasta water should taste salty—not overly salty, but noticeably salty. This is the stage where your pasta takes on its seasoning. Can you add salt later, in the "marriage" of pasta and sauce phase? Yes, but the taste won't be the same. As my Italian friends say, "Ormai è troppo tardi (by then it's too late)."

"Al Dente" versus "Punto Giusto." Cook your pasta to the right point—neither over- nor underdone. This seems obvious. We've all heard about the importance of reaching the "al dente" ideal (the literal translation is "to the tooth," meaning there's some bite left in the pasta that snaps back at you upon biting in). But lots of mistakes are made at this stage of pasta cookery, especially at home in the U.S.

My observation: In the U.S., dried pasta is often overcooked—beyond al dente. And fresh pasta, in a mistaken attempt to turn it out al dente, is very often undercooked.

There will be some who disagree with me, and some who will consider the statement sacrilege, but *fresh pasta is not meant to be served al dente.* Fresh pasta should be cooked through, but not overcooked—we don't want mush. But not undercooked either—to a point insufficient to achieve that silky, soft mouthfeel that makes great fresh pasta a sensual treat. We want to achieve what I call the "punto giusto" (the right point) for fresh pasta.

Make sure your dried pasta is cooked to a point just shy of being done. Taste it to see if there's still

a bit of an almost raw/chewy center. Then toss it in the pan with your sauce and finish cooking it during the emulsification phase.

For fresh pasta, just go a bit longer than you think. You'll see the pasta expand slightly, take on a silky texture, and lose all sense of uncooked flour.

Don't Oversauce. Pasta should not be swimming in sauce. Pasta should be "dressed" with sauce—almost like a salad. You want to achieve a balance between the pasta and the sauce: enough sauce to completely coat the pasta, but no more than that.

"Marry" and Emulsify the Pasta and Sauce Mixture. This may be the most critical step in great pasta cookery. The three individual parts of a pasta dish—the pasta, the sauce, and some pasta cooking water—need to become one perfectly balanced and emulsified whole. This will take some practice. You need to develop a feel for when you've achieved that balanced emulsification—everything incorporated together as a whole, not too dry and not too wet. Work slowly over low heat, stirring to incorporate the three elements and adding more pasta cooking water as needed. Use your senses and your judgment. If your finished dish is too dry, use a bit more sauce and/or cooking water the next time. If your finished dish is watery, use less cooking water and/or continue to cook the mixture longer in the pan until you've evaporated the excess liquid.

RICCARDO

Riccardo Azzato is a force of nature. He epitomizes the small business work ethic that drives so much of the Italian economy. Day in and day out he's in his thoughtfully stocked enoteca (a combination retail wine shop and wine bar) advising serious collectors who visit from all over the world, recommending special-occasion bottles to locals, and preparing light meals for a mixed clientele of tourists, local winemakers, and second homeowners. And he does it all by himself.

Riccardo is a Tuscan transplant. Born and raised in a small town in the Basilicata region of Italy's south, he jumped into the hospitality game at an early age. After a multitude of jobs in restaurants and hotels, and the traditional and obligatory—at that time—military service, he received a call from a Tuscan resort property that changed his life.

Riccardo fell in love with Tuscany, and Chianti in particular. It's become his adopted home, though the draw of his birthplace remains strong and his "Lucano" pride runs unabated in his veins.

Riccardo's shop, La Cantinetta del Chianti, serves as a central gathering place for local wine lovers and "buongustai" (loose translation: foodies) who appreciate his carefully curated selection of wines and specialty food products.

Two dishes—one that I've enjoyed at Riccardo's shop and another that I've been treated to at his home—showcase Riccardo's love for both his birthplace and his "new" home in Tuscany.

ANTIPASTO MISTO "BASILICATA COAST-TO-COAST"
Mixed Antipasto "Basilicata Coast-to-Coast"

The Basilicata region of Italy and, in particular, its capital city of Matera have gained recognition in recent years, in large part due to the opening of the American filmmaker Francis Ford Coppola's luxury hotel and the recognition of the ancient "Sassi" district of Matera as a UNESCO world heritage site. That said, Basilicata is still pretty much under the radar and undiscovered by American tourists.

The region has a rich and diverse food tradition, and Riccardo takes pride in offering this simple but soul-satisfying antipasto plate—named after an Italian film of the same title—as an example of the region's bounty.

During his childhood, Riccardo's parents operated a local butcher shop and partnered with neighbors in the raising of heritage breed pigs. Every winter, when the pigs had reached maturity and conditions were right, they would slaughter and butcher the pigs. Nothing went to waste. Now in retirement, Riccardo's parents continue the annual tradition and produce sausages and assorted salumi similar to those used in this dish.

This is a simple dish—no cooking required. Find a great Italian delicatessen or online specialty food purveyor to source your meats, cheeses, olive oil, and pickled vegetables. And take some time with your presentation. I'm always surprised by how much a dish's visual appeal affects its taste.

You might want to try your hand at home-pickling your vegetables as is done in many Tuscan households. They'll last for months in your refrigerator. The tangy vinegar-laced vegetables offer an appealing contrast to the rich, fatty charcuterie and cheese. This is a great starter course as part of a larger meal.

SERVES 4

12 slices imported prosciutto di Parma

12 slices imported soppressata piccante (spicy)

12 slices imported salame

6 slices fresh buffalo mozzarella

6 slices imported pecorino cheese (Toscano or Romano)

8 ounces (225 g) Italian-style pickled vegetables (giardiniera)

8 slices rustic country-style bread

High-quality extra-virgin olive oil, for dipping or drizzling

1. On a serving platter large enough to accommodate all of the meats, cheeses, and vegetables, arrange all of the ingredients as you please. It's nice to start with the prosciutto, soppressata, and salame at one end, followed by the buffalo mozzarella, pecorino cheese, and finally the pickled vegetables.

2. Toast the bread. A standard toaster works well, but for added flavor, if time and circumstances permit, I think it's preferable to grill the bread. The best grilling method is over a wood or charcoal fire (you may have one going if the antipasto is the first course in a multicourse meal). A grill pan is almost as effective and it's easy to use on your stovetop. Keep a close eye on the bread—you want the slices nicely charred on each side, but not burnt.

3. Serve the plated meats, cheeses, and vegetables with the grilled bread on the side along with a generous amount of extra-virgin olive oil for dipping and drizzling.

Note: It would be next to impossible to secure authentic salumi produced in Basilicata in the U.S. Accordingly, the recipe suggests appropriate substitutions such as prosciutto di Parma for prosciutto Lucano. But the spirit of the dish remains intact.

OSSO BUCO ALLA TOSCANA
Braised Veal Shanks in the Tuscan Style

Osso buco—slow-braised veal shank in a rich sauce—is a well-known and much-loved dish from the northern Lombardia region of Italy. But it's found a place in many other regional Italian cuisines, and Tuscany is no exception. It's a Riccardo favorite and his holds true to the Tuscan version, with a bit more tomato than found in Lombardia.

On a cold winter's evening, it's tough to beat this soulful, comforting dish. The aromas that will fill your kitchen during the three- to four-hour cooking time will have you salivating.

Veal shanks are usually available from artisanal butcher shops on special order and in the meat section of better-quality supermarkets. Look for shanks that are two to three fingers thick; they're best suited to long, slow cooking. When properly braised to perfection, the shanks should be fork-tender. The marrow inside the shank bones can be scooped out by you and your guests with a small spoon or knife to add another layer of flavor and richness to the finished dish. I find that osso buco is best prepared the day before serving and allowed to rest overnight in its sauce. It's even better the next day.

SERVES 4

4 pieces veal shank

Kosher or coarse sea salt and freshly ground black pepper

All-purpose flour, for dusting

4 to 5 tablespoons (60 to 75 ml) best-quality extra-virgin olive oil, plus more as needed

2 carrots, diced into 1-inch (2.5-cm) pieces

2 celery stalks, diced into 1-inch (2.5-cm) pieces

2 yellow onions, diced into 1-inch (2.5-cm) pieces

—continued—

1. Preheat the oven to 300°F (150°C). Place an oven rack in the center position.

2. Season the veal shanks liberally with salt and pepper and then lightly sprinkle the shanks all over with the flour. Shake each shank thoroughly to remove excess flour.

3. In an ovenproof cooking vessel (an enameled cast-iron pot with a lid such as those produced by Le Creuset would be ideal, but a roasting pan can also work) just large enough to accommodate the shanks in a single layer, heat the oil over medium-high heat until you can see the oil beginning to shimmer.

4. Carefully place the shanks into the pan and let them brown on the first side, undisturbed. Resist the temptation to fiddle with or move the shanks—give the heat some time to work its magic.

5. When the first side is nicely browned and crusted, flip the shanks over to the other side and brown. When both sides have been browned, repeat the process on the smaller sides of the shanks so that they are nicely browned all over. Be patient and use your senses. If the meat starts browning too quickly—or worse, starts to burn—lower the heat a bit and add a touch more oil to the pan. This browning step is a critical flavor-building phase. Your patience and diligence will be rewarded. Remove the shanks from the pan and place them on a plate.

—continued—

2 tablespoons (30 ml) high-quality tomato paste

2 cups (480 ml) good-quality red wine, such as Chianti

1 sprig fresh thyme

1 sprig fresh rosemary

1 fresh bay leaf (may substitute dried if fresh is unavailable)

2 to 3 cups (480 to 720 ml) chicken, beef, or vegetable stock, plus more as needed (see A Few Thoughts on Stock, page 51)

1 lemon, cut in half

6. Combine the diced carrot, celery, and onion in the still-warm pan over medium heat. Stir to coat them with the oil in the pan and add some salt and pepper. The vegetables will begin to sweat out their liquid and partially deglaze the bottom of the pan. When the bottom of the pan begins to dry out and the vegetables are starting to take on some color and soften, add the tomato paste to the pan, mixing well to incorporate it into the vegetables, and continue to cook until the mixture caramelizes and begins to leave some residue on the bottom of the pan. At this point, add the red wine to the pan and raise the heat a bit. Reduce until the wine becomes syrupy and almost disappears and its alcohol smell has cooked off.

7. While the wine and vegetable mixture reduces, tie the thyme sprig, rosemary sprig, and bay leaf together in a tight bundle using some kitchen twine. When the mixture has reached the desired syrupy consistency, place the veal shanks back into the pan and then pour in enough stock so that the liquid comes about two-thirds of the way up the shanks. Add the herb bundle and bring everything to a boil.

8. Lower the heat to a slow simmer. Cover the pan tightly with a lid if it has one or with aluminum foil and braise in the oven for 3 to 4 hours, or until the meat is fork-tender and pulls easily away from the shank bones. Check the pot after about 1½ hours to make sure there is still sufficient liquid. Depending on your oven and your local climate, you may experience more or less evaporation of the cooking liquid. Some evaporation is desirable—it will concentrate your sauce. If it looks like the pot is becoming too dry, add a bit more stock and continue with the cooking.

—continued—

OSSO BUCO ALLA TOSCANA
(continued)

9. Remove the shanks from the pot, place them on a warmed plate, and cover with aluminum foil. Remove the herb bundle from the liquid in the pot. At this point, you have two choices: a rustic sauce with the cooked-down vegetables, or a more refined sauce with the vegetables strained out. If you opt for rusticity, place the pan on the stove over medium-high heat and reduce the liquid until it reaches a thicker, saucier consistency. If opting for the more refined version, strain the liquid through a fine-mesh strainer into a smaller saucepan. Place the pan over medium-high heat and reduce to a syrupy consistency.

10. Place one shank on each of four plates. Spoon the reduced sauce generously over the top and add a drizzle of extra-virgin olive oil and a few drops of squeezed lemon. Serve immediately.

Bonus Dish . . . *Piatto di Recupero!*
In the unlikely event you have leftovers, you can easily repurpose the remaining osso buco for a great pasta dish to serve anytime within the next four days. Separate the meat from the shank bones, pull off and discard any cartilage or fibrous parts, and pull the meat apart into bite-size pieces with your hands. Put the meat back into its sauce (this is better done with the "rustic" sauce option described above). Use this mixture as your pasta sauce for a hearty dish of tagliatelle or pappardelle using some pasta cooking water to emulsify and extend the osso buco mixture.

Note: If you prepare the osso buco the day before, you can store it together with its sauce in a sealed container in your refrigerator. Take it out about 2 hours before you plan to serve it. Place it in an ovenproof pan and into a 350°F (180°C) preheated oven for 30 to 45 minutes until heated through.

Make It a Meal: Osso buco is classically paired with a rich saffron risotto (page 50) as an accompaniment. I like the risotto spread out on a serving plate, topped with the osso buco, and drizzled with plenty of sauce. Round it all out with some sautéed greens (page 240).

Wine Pairing: Podere Le Ripi Brunello di Montalcino "Amore e Magia" DOCG 2019. The richness of osso buco demands a bold structured wine such as this Brunello favorite from Montalcino's southeast zone.

RISOTTO SEMPLICE
Basic Risotto

I was thinking about the incredible versatility of risotto—as a side dish or as a hearty main course—and I realized something. There really is no direct translation (at least one that makes sense) for the name of the dish. Literally, *risotto* means "under again"—a reference to the technique of continually submerging the rice during its cooking in repeated doses of stock until it reaches that creamy consistency that makes risotto special. Because the stock is such an important ingredient, the quality of what you use will be a huge factor in how the finished dish tastes. Even perfect cooking technique won't cover up for a poor-quality stock.

Your best option is homemade stock (see A Few Thoughts on Stock, page 51). But if you don't have any on hand, there are acceptable substitutes. Steer away from canned or boxed stocks on supermarket shelves. Sodium content is hard to gauge, and the flavors of these packaged stocks are generally pretty off-putting. Instead, look for stabilized stock concentrates. These are generally sold in sealed plastic containers of various sizes. For risotto, I'd recommend chicken stock concentrate, but veal demi-glace and beef stock concentrates are also available. A small amount of any of these concentrates can be dissolved in hot water to create a quick stock for soups, braises, pan sauces, and risottos. Stored in the refrigerator in a sealed container after opening, these stock concentrates have an almost indefinite shelf life.

SERVES 4

4 cups (960 ml) chicken or vegetable stock

2 tablespoons (30 ml) olive oil

2 tablespoons (30 g) unsalted butter

1 small onion, finely chopped

1½ cups (300 g) Carnaroli rice (may substitute Arborio)

½ cup (120 ml) dry white wine (something you'd be happy to drink)

½ cup (50 g) grated Parmigiano-Reggiano cheese

Kosher or coarse sea salt and freshly ground black pepper

1. In a saucepan, heat the chicken or vegetable broth over low heat.

2. In a separate large saucepan, heat the olive oil and 1 tablespoon (15 g) of the butter over medium heat. Add the finely chopped onion to the pan. Stir with a wooden spoon and sauté until the onions are soft and translucent, 3 to 4 minutes.

3. Add the rice to the pan. Stir well to coat the rice grains with the oil and butter mixture. Toast the rice for about 2 minutes, stirring frequently, until it becomes slightly translucent around the edges.

4. Pour in the white wine. Stir continuously until the wine has been absorbed by the rice and the raw smell of the alcohol has dissipated, 2 to 3 minutes.

5. Add a ladleful of the warm stock to the pan. Stir continuously until the rice has absorbed most of the stock. Add another ladleful of stock to the pan, and once again stir continuously until most of the stock has been absorbed by the rice. Continue this process until the rice is creamy and tender but still slightly firm to the bite. Total cooking time should be 18 to 20 minutes. You may not need to use all of the stock.

—continued—

RISOTTO SEMPLICE
(continued)

6. Once the rice is cooked to the desired consistency, remove the pan from the heat. Add the remaining 1 tablespoon (15 g) of butter and the Parmigiano-Reggiano to the pan. Shake the pan vigorously while simultaneously stirring to incorporate the butter and cheese into the rice. This will create a visible gloss on the rice and help develop a creamy consistency.

7. Season with salt and pepper to taste. Serve immediately.

Variations on the Master Recipe
The basic risotto recipe can be the base for many risotto variations. For saffron risotto, the traditional accompaniment to osso buco, simply add a generous pinch of crushed saffron threads to 1 cup (240 ml) of the warm stock. Allow to steep for at least 5 minutes, stirring occasionally. Add this mixture to the rice early in the cooking process as one of the repeated additions of stock described in step 5 of the recipe. Finish the risotto according to the directions in steps 6 and 7.

For other variations, ingredients like sautéed mushrooms, fresh or frozen peas, blanched asparagus, or halved cherry tomatoes can be added during the final 5 to 7 minutes of cooking. The addition of shrimp, scallops, or parcooked lobster to a saffron or cherry tomato risotto would make for a wonderful main course. It's best to add the seafood during the final 3 to 5 minutes of cooking. Make sure to season your seafood with salt and pepper before adding it to the risotto. Finish the dish with a last-minute scattering of a favorite fresh herb.

A FEW THOUGHTS ON STOCK

Stock is a great thing to have on hand in your kitchen. It adds depth of flavor to braises—like Riccardo's osso buco—or it can be used to produce delicious pan sauces. It's also a good addition to many quick pasta sauces. Chicken, vegetable, veal, and beef stock concentrates are all readily available in supermarkets and from specialty food purveyors. These products come in condensed gelatin or solid cube forms that are reconstituted in hot water. But no question, homemade stock is best. It can be prepared in batches beforehand, frozen, and used as and when needed.

I won't give you an exhaustive tutorial on stock-making. There are other places you can turn to for that. But a delicious stock can be easily put together. A leftover roast chicken carcass—check. Aromatic vegetable scraps, maybe carrots, onions, leeks, and celery—check. Add it all to a stock pot, cover with water, and bring it up to a low boil on your stovetop. Lower the heat as far down as you can and let the pot gurgle away at a mere whispering simmer for a couple of hours, periodically skimming off any impurities that rise to the top. Let cool and strain through a fine-mesh strainer.

MARCELLA

Friends often ask us how we're sure our home in Chianti is secure and cared for when we're away. The answer: Marcella Cortigiani. Marcella is what the locals call a "Gaiolese DOC" ("DOC" stands for "denominazione di origine controllata," the designation that guarantees an Italian wine actually comes from a specific place). Born and raised in Gaiole, she's lived here her entire life.

Marcella's parents were part of the last generation of Tuscan sharecroppers—hardworking, industrious people who tended to the large landholdings of wealthy Tuscan aristocrats in exchange for housing and a portion of what they produced. They farmed, raised animals, produced olive oil, and made wine. These were can-do people who made the most of what they had and wasted nothing. Their children worked alongside them.

We met Marcella shortly after acquiring our home in Gaiole. Retired from a job with the Italian government, she was restless at home and searching for a way to reconnect with her agrarian roots. She's been with us ever since.

Marcella's energy is boundless and her love for Chianti contagious. She's a master gardener, is an olive tree expert and pruner, and has admirably tried her hand as an amateur stonemason at Casa Bersani. There's no job too big or too small for this dynamo of a woman.

Of course, she cooks too. Every day at 1:00 p.m. sharp, Marcella's two sons and extended family gather at her home for the traditional midday lunch break. The food is simple but satisfying. Everyone leaves content and fortified for the rest of the workday. On special occasions—a birthday, a wedding shower, a holiday, or a large family gathering on a leisurely Sunday afternoon—Marcella prepares her pasta al forno, as Tuscans often call lasagna. It's a rich, comforting dish that is always a crowd-pleaser.

LA PASTA AL FORNO DELLA MARCELLA
Oven-Baked Lasagna Marcella-Style

Lasagna as we think of it in the U.S.—stacked high, heavy with red sauce, and stuffed with everything from meatballs and sausage to ricotta and mozzarella cheeses—has nothing in common with the real deal in Italy. Yes, a classic lasagna is filling and rich. But it's a far simpler, and to me far tastier, dish than the Americanized version.

This recipe seems daunting—there are three critical elements: a rich Tuscan ragu, handmade pasta, and a creamy béchamel sauce. They are all pretty simple, but they do take time. Plan ahead. Maybe make your ragu the day before to break things up. In any event, don't shy away from trying your hand at this classic recipe.

SERVES 6

FOR THE RAGU

4 carrots

4 celery stalks

6 medium-large red onions

¼ cup (60 ml) high-quality extra-virgin olive oil, plus more as needed

2 pounds (940 g) 80% to 85% lean ground beef

2 cups (480 ml) good-quality red wine, such as Chianti

1 sprig fresh rosemary

1 sprig fresh sage

1 fresh bay leaf (may substitute dried if unavailable)

1 (28-oz/800-g) can high-quality whole San Marzano tomatoes, crushed by hand

Kosher or coarse sea salt and freshly ground black pepper

2 cups (480 ml) chicken or beef stock or water

–continued–

To make the ragu:

1. In a food processor fitted with a metal blade, individually process the carrots, celery, and onions to a very fine minced consistency. Alternatively, you can hand-cut the vegetables into a fine dice.

2. Pour about ½ inch (1.3 cm) of extra-virgin olive oil into a large Dutch oven, casserole, or pot large enough to accommodate the vegetables and ground beef. Heat the olive oil over medium-high heat until just shimmering. Add the minced carrot, celery, and onion and stir to coat them with the oil. Decrease the heat to low and slowly cook the vegetables. Initially, the vegetables will release their liquids and turn translucent. As the cooking slowly continues, this "soffritto" mixture will begin to take on color and eventually reach an almost bronze-like tone. This may take up to 30 minutes or more. Be patient. This caramelization process is one of the keys to developing great flavor in your ragu.

3. When the soffritto has reached the "bronze stage," add the ground beef and stir thoroughly to mix the meat well with the soffritto. Raise the heat slightly and allow the meat to brown all over, stirring occasionally to ensure even cooking. A little bit of caramelization and browning and meat sticking to the bottom of the pan is a good thing at this stage, but be careful not to let it burn.

—continued—

FOR THE BÉCHAMEL

8 ounces (475 g) unsalted butter

8 ounces (475 g) all-purpose flour

4 to 5 cups (1 to 1.25 L) whole milk

FOR THE PASTA

1 portion freshly made pasta sheets (page 58), rolled out to a standard number 6 thickness, squared off, and cut into lengths a bit smaller than the baking dish that will hold the lasagna

Parmigiano-Reggiano cheese, as needed for the lasagna assembly

4. Add the red wine and deglaze the bottom of the pot, scraping up all the brown bits with a wooden spoon. Allow the wine to bubble away and reduce until all that remains is a syrupy glaze and the harsh alcohol smell has burned off.

5. Tie the rosemary, sage, and bay leaf together neatly with kitchen twine. Add the tomatoes and the herb bundle to the pan and give it a stir. Season at this point with salt and pepper—don't add too much; you'll taste for seasoning later and can always add more, but you can't take it away. Add 1 cup (240 ml) of the stock, if using, or water.

6. Mix thoroughly and bring the pot up to a boil. Decrease the heat to the lowest possible setting and let the ragu slowly simmer for 3 hours. Stir from time to time and check to see if the liquid has mostly evaporated. Add more stock or water a little at a time as necessary to keep things fairly liquid. By the end, you want a fairly dry consistency, with just the tomatoes, meat, and olive oil providing structure to the ragu. Taste for seasoning and add more salt and/or pepper as needed.

7. If you are preparing the ragu in advance, store it in an airtight plastic container in your refrigerator. The ragu will keep for up to 5 days refrigerated. Remove the ragu from the refrigerator about 1 hour prior to assembling the lasagna. Any leftover ragu can also be frozen for future use. Frozen ragu will keep well for up to 2 months in the freezer.

To make the béchamel:

8. Melt the butter in a medium saucepan over low heat. Add the flour and stir to incorporate until the mixture reaches the consistency of loose, wet sand, about 2 minutes. Do not allow the mixture to take on a lot of color—we don't want a dark Cajun-style roux—we're after the classic creamy-white béchamel of French origins.

9. Raise the heat to medium-low, add half the milk to the pan, and stir vigorously and constantly with a wire whisk to incorporate the milk with the butter/flour mixture, doing your best to eliminate lumps.

10. As the mixture thickens, continue adding milk gradually, while stirring with your whisk. You're looking for a creamy, silky consistency without lumps. When it reaches the proper stage of "doneness," the béchamel should run from the tines of the whisk with the consistency of pancake batter. Keep in mind that the béchamel will thicken up a bit as it cools. It's easiest to work with when still warm.

To assemble the lasagna:

11. Preheat the oven to 400°F (200°C).

12. Bring a large pot of salted water to a boil over high heat.

13. In a large bowl or storage container, prepare an ice bath.

14. Cook the fresh pasta sheets in the boiling salted water, stirring occasionally, for 3 to 4 minutes, just to the point where they are starting to swell or expand a bit. Remove the pasta sheets with a spider strainer and plunge them into the ice bath to stop the cooking process. Once cooled—just a couple of minutes—remove the pasta sheets and place them on paper towels or kitchen towels to dry and remove excess water. Pat the tops of the sheets dry as well.

15. In a heavy-bottomed baking dish (the Le Creuset models are ideal), spoon a thin layer of the ragu onto the bottom. Cover with a single layer of the fresh pasta, cutting the pasta sheets as necessary to fit the dimensions of your baking dish. Some overlapping is okay. Add another thin layer of ragu on top of the pasta. Top the ragu with a generous slathering of béchamel. Top the béchamel with a generous grating of Parmigiano-Reggiano. Repeat this layering two more times for a total of three layers of pasta, ragu, béchamel, and Parmigiano. Keep in mind that balance is key. If you are a bit sparing with the ragu and a bit more generous with the béchamel, you will achieve a beautiful, rich, final consistency.

16. Add one final layer of pasta to the top of the lasagna. Slather the pasta generously once again with béchamel, a few dabs of ragu, and grate a generous amount of Parmigiano on top. Depending on the quantities you've prepared and the dimensions of your baking dish, you may or may not have leftover ragu and/or béchamel that can be stored and used for another purpose.

17. Cover the baking dish with aluminum foil and bake for 30 minutes. Remove the aluminum foil and continue baking until the lasagna has turned golden on top with some charred edges and spots and is bubbling, 15 to 20 minutes longer.

18. Allow the lasagna to rest for at least 15 minutes before cutting and serving.

Note: You can assemble the lasagna earlier in the day (or even the day before) and store it in your refrigerator. If you go this route, remove the lasagna from the refrigerator at least 1 hour before you plan to bake it, and proceed as directed in Step 17.

Make It a Meal: A rich lasagna like this one could be served in small portions as a hearty appetizer followed by grilled meats (pages 67 and 187). Or, make it the star of your meal in larger portions preceded by a simple salad (page 199).

Wine Pairing: Castello di Ama Chianti Classico DOCG 2018. A classic dish like pasta al forno is best enjoyed with a straightforward expression of Sangiovese like this one from one of Chianti's legendary producers.

MY WAY WITH FRESH PASTA

I've made a lot of fresh pasta in my day. It really isn't as difficult as it seems. If you persist—and as your senses begin to know when you've reached that point of perfect dough consistency—you'll become adept and you'll never accept store-bought fresh pasta in your kitchen again.

There are many variations of fresh pasta recipes. Some call for the use of only egg yolks and flour; others whole eggs; yet others may suggest the addition of some water or olive oil. But in the end, all these approaches have one common principle: fresh pasta is the combination of flour and liquid to produce a dough with just enough elasticity for proper shaping or cutting. Too soft and sticky and your dough will not roll out properly. Too dry and rigid and it will be very difficult to work with and may even break apart. As with many things in the kitchen, balance is key.

This is my standard fresh pasta recipe and approach.

MAKES ABOUT 1½ POUNDS (680 G) PASTA

4 to 5 cups (about 1 lb/455 g) doppio zero "00" flour

2 large whole eggs

4 large egg yolks

1 scant teaspoon high-quality extra-virgin olive oil

Pour the flour onto your work surface (which might be a large wooden cutting board or even just your clean kitchen counter). Using your hands, make a well in the center of the flour pile, pushing the flour outward to form a shallow but fully enclosed "volcano." (See photo #1.)

Place the whole eggs and egg yolks in the flour volcano. (See photo #2.)

Add just a touch—no more than a scant teaspoon—of extra-virgin olive oil to the well with the egg mixture.

Using a fork, mix or beat the egg and oil mixture while gradually incorporating a bit of flour from the innermost part of the volcano well into the mixture. Work slowly and with confidence, making sure to keep the walls of the well intact so the liquid doesn't seep out onto your work surface. (See photo #3.)

Gradually, the egg mixture will begin to thicken up as the flour is steadily incorporated. When the danger of the liquid seeping out has passed (the mixture will have reached a slurry-like consistency), begin to push some of the flour off to the side to keep it available for later incorporation. (See photos #4 and #5.)

Continue to work more flour into the slurry, using a dough scraper and "cutting" the flour into the forming mass to incorporate it well. (See photos #6 and #7.)

Having passed the slurry stage into the more pliable dough-like stage, begin to knead the dough with your hands and continue incorporating flour in the process. Press down into the dough with the heel of your palm, fold the dough over onto itself, give it a quarter turn, and repeat the process. (See photos #8 and #9.) Continue kneading and adding flour until you've produced a shiny dough ball of even consistency. (See photo #10.) Depending on the humidity on any given day, as well as the size and consistency of the eggs you use, you may or may not use all of the flour to achieve the desired consistency.

Lightly dust the dough ball with flour and place it in a zip-top plastic bag, taking care to push out as much of the air in the bag as possible. Place the dough in the refrigerator and allow to rest for at least 30 minutes.

Take the dough out of the fridge and remove it from the plastic bag. Cut the dough ball into three equal pieces. Put two of the balls back into the plastic bag to keep them from drying out and developing a crusted exterior while you work with the third ball.

Warm the dough ball between your hands and begin to work it into a flat disk. The warmth of your hands will help the dough relax and become a bit more pliable as you begin to work it.

Using a rolling pin, further flatten and extend the dough disk, working it into a somewhat rectangular shape about ¼ inch (6 mm) thick. Make sure it's not too wide for your pasta machine.

Put the flattened dough through the widest setting of a pasta machine. Fold the dough over onto itself, lengthwise, bringing each of the two shorter sides over onto themselves in the center of the dough and then flattening it by hand.

Put the folded dough through the widest setting of the pasta machine again and then repeat two more times. The multiple passings of the dough through the machine will help develop the dough's structure and elasticity.

Adjust your pasta machine to the next narrowest setting and pass the dough through twice. Continue in the same manner, narrowing the pasta machine setting each time, until you reach the desired pasta thickness for your recipe (generally setting 5 or 6—thicker for noodles, thinner for stuffed pastas and multiple layered pastas like lasagna). If at any time during the rolling process the dough seems to be a bit too sticky, dust it lightly on both sides with some flour before proceeding with the next pass through the pasta machine. Lay the finished pasta sheet out on a lightly floured surface to dry just a bit.

Repeat steps 10 through 14 with the two remaining dough balls.

Cut the finished pasta sheets into your desired shape according to the specific pasta recipe's directions.

Note: for recipes such as tagliatelle, fettuccine, maltagliati, and the like, figure about 4 ounces (120 g) of fresh pasta per serving; i.e., a 1-pound (455-g) batch should serve four people.

1

2

3

6

7

8

4

5

9

10

BUCA DELL'ORAFO

The city of Florence lies just one hour north of our home in Chianti. It's become a favorite escape when we've had a bit too much countryside tranquility and we're longing for the hum and bustle of a big city. Florence has it all—world-renowned museums, high fashion, Renaissance-era architectural masterpieces, and a history marked by Tuscan genius and political intrigue. And, of course, there's the food . . .

You have to be careful about food in Florence. It's a tourist city, overwhelmed certain times of the year by hordes of visitors following impersonal tour guides like lemmings, faces turned up toward the sky. An entire industry of tourist-trap eateries has sprung up to feed these masses, and I'm sorry to say that much of what comes out of them is at best bland and at worst inedible. It is certainly not true Florentine cuisine, with its rich history and deeply satisfying, straightforward, powerful flavors.

But great Florentine cooking is alive and well in Florence. You just have to know where to look.

Ristorante Buca dell'Orafo is the kind of place you've passed by a hundred times and either missed or, just as likely, hesitated to try. Its quirky location—hidden under a portico in a tiny subterranean space—adds to the mystery. *Is this a tourist trap?* you might wonder, as it's just steps from the Ponte Vecchio. *Is it a private club?* It can seem that way. It's tough to get a reservation unless you're a regular or willing to eat at 7:30 p.m. as part of the "tourist seating" (something a Florentine would never consider).

In my view, Ristorante Buca dell'Orafo is one of the very best traditional trattorias in Florence. It's got character. It's got history. And it's got killer food.

I first discovered "Buca" in 2008. We'd rented an apartment just around the corner from the restaurant on Via Lambertesca. Our two daughters were attending school in Florence that fall—one as a sixth-grader at the International School of Florence and the other doing a college semester abroad. We'd stay in the city during the week and head to Chianti on the weekends. An acquaintance in Gaiole mentioned the Buca and urged us to check it out.

I'd passed by the restaurant numerous times. It certainly didn't look like anything special. But I was curious. So, on several occasions, I popped my head in to ask for a dinner reservation only to be told each time, "Sorry, we're completely full. Try again." On my fourth or fifth failed attempt, the guy at the door, wanting to show me some pity and also some respect for my persistence, suggested that I try at lunchtime. "It's quieter," he explained.

Finally, on a brisk autumn day—one of those days that's perfect for a hearty lunch and some daytime wine consumption—Cyndy and I, together with our daughter Kristin, had our first meal at the Buca. A heaping platter of cured Tuscan meats; crostini slathered with the traditional Florentine chicken liver pâté; plates of handmade maltagliati pasta tossed with a rich Tuscan ragu; and groppa scaloppata, thin, rare slices of grilled beef cut from the hindquarter, finished with emerald green extra-virgin olive oil that had been dressed with peppercorns, rosemary sprigs, and shaved pecorino cheese; all washed down with a bottle of Chianti Classico Riserva. We were hooked. We became regulars. We got in for dinner!

Buca has been serving traditional Florentine and regional Tuscan cuisine since 1945. The owner and chef—Giordano Monni—is a fanatic about sourcing the best possible ingredients and treating them in a way that exalts their flavors.

This book would not be complete without a section dedicated to our friends at the Buca, and the dishes they love to cook.

GIORDANO

Our friend and Buca dell'Orafo chef/owner, Giordano Monni, is faithfully carrying the torch of traditional Florentine trattoria cooking. In a tourist city filled with mediocre food, the Buca remains true to its roots: quality ingredients, attention to detail, and bold flavors.

If you want to try one of the city's best versions of the famous bistecca alla fiorentina—a thick-cut Tuscan porterhouse steak grilled and finished with olive oil and rosemary—the Buca's got you covered. But Giordano also offers, in his quest to showcase Florentine cooking ingenuity, less-prized cuts that you won't find elsewhere. And he treats them in a way that brings out their best. There's no better example than Giordano's groppa scaloppata, a delicious alternative to the ubiquitous fiorentina.

GROPPA SCALOPPATA CON PECORINO FRESCO E PROFUMI

Grilled and Sliced Top Round of Beef with Fresh Pecorino Cheese and Tuscan Herbs

The "groppa" cut of beef comes from the animal's hindquarter and would generally be labeled in U.S. supermarkets and butcher shops as "rump" or "top round." These cuts are commonly used in Italy for roasting but, as demonstrated in this dish, can also be great when grilled, sliced thin against the grain of the meat, and dressed with olive oil and aromatics. Here's how it's done at the Buca.

SERVES 4 TO 6

1 (1½- to 2-lb/680- to 910-g) rump or top round roast

Kosher or coarse sea salt and freshly ground black pepper

½ cup (120 ml) high-quality extra-virgin olive oil

10 whole peppercorns, lightly crushed

3 sprigs fresh rosemary

Pecorino toscano cheese (for this dish, I recommend a pecorino on the fresher side as opposed to longer aged versions)

1. Light a wood or charcoal fire in your outdoor grill (if an outdoor grill is unavailable, preheat a ridged grill pan over high heat on your stovetop).

2. Trim off any excess fat and/or silver skin from the surface of the meat. The meat will be seared over medium-high heat. Accordingly, to make sure that the internal temperature of the meat can reach a beautiful medium-rare, you may want to cut the roast in half lengthwise (through the center) to create two thinner pieces. Use your judgment. If the meat looks too thick, it probably is. If it seems just right—go with it.

3. Season the meat generously with salt and pepper all over.

4. Grill the meat over medium-high heat. Turn occasionally to ensure the meat is evenly seared on all sides, but don't rush it. If you try to turn the meat too soon, it will stick to your grill. Wait until the meat has seared sufficiently to release easily from the cooking surface. Your target is a medium-rare internal temperature, 7 to 8 minutes total cooking time. Check the internal temperature with a meat thermometer and remove the meat from the grill when the thickest part of the roast has reached 125°F (50°C). It will continue to cook as it rests on your cutting board, eventually getting to 130 to 135°F (55 to 57°C).

5. Allow the meat to rest on a cutting board for 10 minutes.

—continued—

GROPPA SCALOPPATA CON PECORINO FRESCO E PROFUMI *(continued)*

6. While the meat is resting, combine the extra-virgin oil, peppercorns, and rosemary in a large sauté pan and slowly warm it up over low heat. Bring the mixture to a very slow, gentle simmer, allowing the flavors to meld and the rosemary to just slightly wilt. Turn off the heat and set the mixture aside while you carve the meat.

7. Carve the meat into very thin slices, cutting against the grain. Place the slices into the sauté pan with the olive oil mixture. Place the pan over low heat and stir the meat and aromatics together. (Make sure the pan is just warm; you don't actually want to cook the meat any further, but rather simply marry the ingredients and barely heat them through.) Turn off the heat.

8. Portion the meat out onto warmed serving plates and spoon some of the aromatic mixture over each. Using a vegetable peeler, shave three or four generous ribbons of the pecorino cheese on top of the meat. Serve immediately.

Make It a Meal: At the Buca, most diners find it impossible not to add an order of fried zucchini flowers to this dish (page 91).

Wine Pairing: Let's splurge! Marchesi Antinori Tignanello IGT Toscana 2016. Antinori's "Tignanello" was a Super Tuscan pioneer as one of the first to combine indigenous Sangiovese with Cabernet Sauvignon grapes.

PENNE CON SALSICCIA E CAVOLO NERO
Penne with Sausage and Tuscan Black Kale

When you first start to feel a fresh autumn nip in the Tuscan air, usually sometime in late October or early November, it's a sure sign that cavolo nero (black Tuscan kale) is beginning to push up from gardens across the countryside. It's best known as the key ingredient in the famous Tuscan soup ribollita (more to come about that on page 76), but it also takes a bow in many other fall dishes.

At the Buca, Giordano prepares a delicious mixture of Tuscan sausage, cavolo nero, and a touch of tomato, which he uses to dress toothsome penne pasta. If you want something lighter, just skip the sausage. Or if you want to create a great appetizer rather than a full pasta course, either mixture can be spooned on top of slices of grilled country bread and drizzled with extra-virgin olive oil—a great start to a hearty fall meal.

SERVES 4

12 ounces (340 g) high-quality Italian sausage (hot or sweet or a combination of both)

½ cup (120 ml) high-quality extra-virgin olive oil, plus more as needed

2 or 3 bunches Tuscan black kale

1 garlic clove

¼ cup (60 ml) hand-crushed high-quality whole San Marzano tomatoes

Kosher or coarse sea salt and freshly ground black pepper

1 pound (455 g) penne rigate pasta

Parmigiano-Reggiano cheese

1. Bring a large pot of water to a boil over high heat.

2. Score each piece of sausage with the tip of a knife to create a slit in the casing and remove the meat from the casings. Heat ¼ cup (60 ml) of the olive oil in a large sauté pan over medium-low-heat. Raise the heat to medium, place the sausages in the pan, and sauté, stirring and breaking the meat up into small pieces with a wooden spoon as the meat cooks, until the meat is browned all over. Remove the browned sausage meat from the pan and allow it to cool in a bowl until it can be handled. Working in batches and using a chef's knife, cut the sausage into smaller uniform pieces, about ½ inch (1.3 cm) in size. Set aside.

3. Remove and discard the center stems from each kale leaf. Chop the kale leaves into uniform bite-size pieces.

4. In a large heavy Dutch oven, medium stockpot, or large sauté pan (you could use the same pan you used to cook the sausage), heat the remaining ¼ cup (60 ml) of olive oil over medium heat. Add the garlic clove, allow it to take on just a bit of color, and then begin adding the chopped kale in batches, stirring as you go, until all the kale is in the pan and has begun to wilt and cook down.

—continued—

PENNE CON SALSICCIA E CAVOLO NERO *(continued)*

5. Slowly cook the kale, adding a bit of liquid if the pan becomes too dry (stock if you have it; water if you don't), until it has softened considerably, about 10 minutes.

6. Add the crushed tomatoes, season to taste with salt and pepper, stir well, and continue cooking the mixture for another 6 to 8 minutes. Add the diced sausage to the pan, mix to incorporate everything together, and remove from the heat.

7. Add a generous amount of salt to the pot of boiling water. Toss in the penne and cook until al dente (see Some Thoughts on Pasta, page 36).

8. Just before the penne is finished cooking, reheat the sausage and kale mixture over medium heat, adding several spoonfuls of the pasta cooking water as you do so. When the pasta is cooked, remove it from the pot with a spider strainer or large slotted spoon, add it directly to the saucepan and "marry" the pasta with the condiment (see Some Thoughts on Pasta, page 36). Add more pasta water, if necessary, to emulsify and create the desired consistency in the final dish. Turn off the heat, add some grated Parmigiano-Reggiano cheese and a glug of olive to the pan, and mix to incorporate.

9. Portion into warmed pasta bowls and serve immediately with more Parmigiano-Reggiano on the side.

Bonus Dish . . . *Piatto di Recupero!*
If you have leftover sauce, it makes for a great bruschetta topping. Remove it from the refrigerator an hour or so before you plan to use it. Allow the sauce to come to room temperature. Grill or toast several pieces of sliced rustic country bread, top with the leftover sauce, drizzle generously with extra-virgin olive oil, and serve immediately. Paired with a small side salad, this could be dinner.

Wine Pairing: Poggerino Chianti Classico Riserva DOCG Bugialla 2019. This Chianti riserva from the Radda UGA (Unità Geografica Aggiuntiva; translation: "Additional Geographic Unit," as regional subzones are now known throughout Chianti) shows the progress and potential of this zone, which in recent years has begun to attract much-deserved attention.

SAVERIO

When I tell friends that the famous Clint Eastwood film *A Fistful of Dollars* was conceived, written, and produced in Italy (though filmed in Spain), they find it hard to believe. What could be more American than classic western films, with their iconic portrayals of rugged lawmen, gunslingers, and tumbleweed-strewn towns terrorized by ruthless gangs?

But the fact is, throughout the mid-'60s and early '70s, Italy was a dominant force in the production of so-called Spaghetti Westerns—films based on the legends of the western U.S. but produced in Italy and Spain far more cheaply than could be done in the U.S. Men like the Italian film director Sergio Leone, who produced and directed *A Fistful of Dollars*, and Ennio Morricone, who wrote the musical score for the film, built the foundation of their careers in the genre. It's a cultural phenomenon that leaves you shaking your head and smiling. Italian ingenuity and creativity at work.

Fast-forward to today. In the wilderness of coastal Tuscany, cult followers of the Spaghetti Western genre are making new films. They're working on shoestring budgets aided by the latest cinematographic technology but sparing no expense in seeking out original costumes and props. My good friend Saverio Monni, the brother of Giordano of Buca dell'Orafo fame, is one of these new-wave Italian western actors.

By day, Saverio is a professional waiter. He's charismatic, passionate about life, mischievous, and just a little bit crazy in that good-crazy kinda way. In the evenings, having earned the right after thirty years of hard work to skip the Buca's nightly dinner service, he's either spending time with his wife and daughter or rehearsing for his next theatrical production. Acting is his passion.

Over the years as customers of the Buca, Saverio has introduced us to some Florentine classics. Here are two of his favorites.

BACCELLI FRESCHI E PECORINO
Fresh Fava Beans with Pecorino Cheese

In the springtime, fava beans—known as baccelli in Tuscan dialect—are overflowing on farmers' stands in Florence's open-air markets. Our favorite place to food shop on a day trip to the city is the Sant' Ambrogio market on the eastern edge of Florence's historic center. It's a lively, colorful place with both outdoor and indoor vendors and a mind-bending selection of high-quality products. Springtime offerings include peas, asparagus, artichokes, and fava beans.

This dish is less about cooking and more about honoring the season and the product. Every ingredient has to be perfect to achieve the desired result—a classic "the-whole-is-greater-than-the-sum-of-the-parts" deal. If you can source beautiful spring favas, and combine them with young, fresh pecorino cheese and great olive oil, you will really be surprised by the jolt of flavor this simple appetizer packs.

SERVES 4

2 pounds (910 g) fresh spring fava beans

1 pound (455 g) fresh, semisoft pecorino cheese

High-quality extra-virgin olive oil

Kosher or coarse sea salt and freshly ground black pepper

1 lemon, cut in half (optional)

1. Remove the fava beans from their long outer shells and place them in a bowl. Try to buy super-fresh favas that will be on the smaller side. You won't need to bother with removing the outer skin of the individual bean pods, which can be a long and tedious process. The younger favas' outer skin is delicate and won't detract in any way from the taste and texture of the dish.

2. Cut the pecorino cheese into small cubes about the same size as the fava beans. Make sure to buy very young, very fresh, semisoft pecorino cheese. Otherwise, the finished dish won't be what it should. Aged pecorino is far too strong and dry for the delicate favas. Place the cubed cheese into the bowl with the fava beans.

3. Drizzle the fava bean/pecorino mixture with a generous amount of extra-virgin olive oil, season to taste with salt (use a light hand here, as the pecorino already brings a fair amount of saltiness to the dish), add several generous grinds of fresh black pepper, and, if you want to add a bit of freshness/acidity to offset the richness of the cheese, a squeeze or two of fresh lemon juice. Lightly toss everything together to combine and "marry" the ingredients as you would a salad. Portion out onto individual serving plates and serve.

Make It a Meal: This is a great light starter with almost any main course you might choose.

LA RIBOLLITA
Tuscan Black Kale and Bean Soup

No book about regional Tuscan cuisine would be complete without a recipe for the classic ribollita. It's a hearty vegetable soup with cannellini beans and cavolo nero taking the starring roles. Once it's finished, the soup is usually fortified by the addition of Tuscan bread. And in the most traditional renditions, it's left to cool and meld together overnight, then reheated in a pan (the literal translation of *ribollita* is "reboiled") just before serving.

Personally, I prefer my ribollita without the bread, and many restaurants offer the dish "con or senza pane," with or without bread. Of course, purists will say that without the bread it's no longer ribollita, it's just a "minestra" (plain old soup). But, hey—it's all about personal preference.

SERVES 6

3 medium carrots

4 medium zucchini

3 medium yellow onions

4 medium celery stalks

½ cup (120 ml) high-quality extra-virgin olive oil

2 to 3 tablespoons (30 to 45 g) butter

3 large bunches Tuscan black kale (cavolo nero)

6 (1-lb/455-g) cans cannellini or navy beans (preferably packed in their own juices)

4 or 5 cherry tomatoes

5 cups (1.2 L) chicken or vegetable stock or water

Kosher or coarse sea salt and freshly ground black pepper

3 or 4 slices 2- or 3-day-old rustic country bread (optional)

Parmigiano-Reggiano cheese (optional)

1. Cut the carrots, zucchini, onions, and celery into equal bite-size pieces. Place the vegetables into a stockpot large enough to hold the finished soup. Add the olive oil and butter to the pot. Warm the contents of the pot over medium-low heat. You want the vegetables to begin to soften and become translucent—they should not caramelize or take on color.

2. Meanwhile, chop the Tuscan kale into 1-inch (2.5-cm) wide strips. Add the chopped kale to the pot and stir to combine. Continue cooking the mixture until the kale has wilted and melded in with the rest of the vegetables.

3. Drain and rinse the beans thoroughly. Add two-thirds of the beans to the vegetable mixture and stir well to combine. Quarter the cherry tomatoes and add them to the pot. Add the stock to the pot until the liquid just covers the vegetables. Bring the pot to a boil and then lower the heat to a steady simmer. Add salt and pepper to taste.

4. Place the remaining one-third of the beans in a bowl or tall container and puree to a smooth consistency with an immersion blender. If you don't have an immersion blender, you can use a regular blender or a food processor. Or you can just break the beans up and mash them using a fork or other utensil. Add the bean puree to the pot.

—continued—

LA RIBOLLITA
(continued)

5. Allow the entire mixture to simmer slowly until the vegetables and kale are soft and the liquid has taken on the consistency and taste of a broth, about 1 hour. If the soup seems too thick, add a bit more water. If it seems too thin, continue to cook and reduce the liquid a bit longer. Taste for seasoning and add more salt and pepper if needed. If serving without the addition of bread, ladle the soup into individual serving bowls, drizzle with extra-virgin olive oil, and grate some Parmigiano-Reggiano cheese on top, as an option.

6. If using bread, remove and discard the crust and cut the remaining interior crumb of the bread into small pieces. Add the bread to the soup and stir to combine well. Continue to cook until the bread has broken down, incorporated itself into the soup and thickened the mixture. Ladle the soup into individual serving bowls, drizzle with extra-virgin olive oil, and grate some Parmigiano-Reggiano cheese on top, if using.

Note: The soup can also be cooled, stored in the refrigerator overnight, and reheated in a pot the next day. The "with bread" version is also sometimes reheated in individual portions over high heat in a nonstick pan to produce a crustier result.

Make It a Meal: There's nothing like a big, stand-alone bowl of this soul-satisfying soup on a cold winter's evening. The only other thing you'll want are some grilled slices of country bread smothered in olive oil (page 179) and a glass of your favorite red wine.

SAVERIO ON TWO WHEELS

When Saverio is not working or acting, he's usually on his bicycle. Italians are crazy for cycling. While soccer is the undisputed king of Italian sports, one could easily make the case that cycling is next in national popularity. On Saturday mornings throughout Chianti, groups of Italian men can be seen cruising along the steep, winding roads of the Tuscan countryside at hair-raising speeds, many aboard tricked-out racing bicycles that can exceed $10,000 USD in value.

Saverio takes his love of the sport and his fitness obsession to another level by commuting by bicycle from his home on the outskirts of Florence to the Buca every day—12.5 miles (20 km) each way. That's more than 25 miles (40 km) a day. All that riding demands sustenance. And not many dishes pack a better punch of satisfying sustenance than la ribollita.

KARLY

About two years or so into our tenure as regulars at the Buca, we were at lunch one afternoon when Saverio pulled me aside on my way to the restroom and said, "I want you to meet someone." He called into the tiny kitchen and a young woman in her mid to late twenties emerged with a huge smile on her face and sweat beading down her forehead from the 90°F (32°C)-plus temperature emanating from the six-burner stove and live grill inside.

Karly Siciliano—a second-generation Italian-American from Washington, D.C.—had arrived in Florence two years earlier to chase her dream of becoming a professional chef and learning to do it the Italian way. She'd spent time after university searching for her passion in life, and wherever the search led it kept circling back to the kitchen.

On a whim, Karly enrolled in Florence's well-regarded Apicius cooking school, packed up her belongings, and moved to the City of Art. She knew no one in Florence. She didn't speak Italian. Pretty gutsy stuff.

Karly had recently finished her course of training and earned her degree from Apicius. During her studies, she'd met Giordano, who was a member of the school's part-time adjunct faculty. Recognizing Karly's work ethic, skill in the kitchen, and innate sense for building flavors, Giordano offered her a job in the Buca's kitchen. She immediately accepted.

Over the course of four years at the Buca—arriving early every morning to prep for lunch service and returning in the evening for the dinner rush—Karly rose through the male-dominated ranks to become Giordano's trusted chef de cuisine. Not only did she master the Buca classics, but she also created a few new ones of her own.

COSCIA D'ANATRA CONFIT
Duck Leg Confit

When you dine at the Buca, you're presented with a paper menu that's printed each day. On the long list of antipasti, primi, secondi, and dolci, which includes wittily reimagined category names such as "Animali d'Aqua" (water animals) in place of "Pesce" (fish), you'll find some dishes that are underlined for emphasis. These are dishes from Florentine tradition. The others—equally delicious and intriguing—come from other parts of the Italian peninsula and, occasionally, from other parts of the world (think shrimp curry).

Duck leg confit, one of my favorite guilty pleasures, is something you expect to find in a dark Parisian bistro, not in a Florentine trattoria. But here it is, one of several additions to the Buca repertoire that Karly's culinary nudging moved onto the menu.

This is a dish that requires more planning and patience than cooking technique. You need to find whole duck legs; you need to cure them overnight; and, if possible, you should find some rendered duck fat in which to "confit" the legs. Because rendered duck fat can be very difficult to source, you can substitute a high-quality extra-virgin olive oil.

You can confit the legs several days in advance, wipe them dry, and finish them at the moment of service. Don't be intimidated. Try this. Your guests will be wowed. Serve with a small side salad of baby greens dressed simply with a lemon vinaigrette.

SERVES 8

8 whole duck legs (drumstick and thigh attached)

Kosher or coarse sea salt

8 sprigs fresh rosemary

12 garlic cloves, crushed

5 to 6 cups (1.2 to 1.45 L) rendered duck fat or high-quality extra-virgin olive oil

1. Place 4 of the duck legs in the bottom of a plastic storage container or another nonreactive container just large enough to accommodate the legs.

2. Generously season the duck legs with salt. Strew half of the rosemary sprigs and half the crushed garlic cloves over the top of the duck legs and press down with your hands to compress everything together. Place the remaining 4 duck legs on top of everything, and repeat the process.

3. Cover with plastic wrap or paper towels and place a heavy weight—could be two bricks, a heavy saucepan, or a couple jars of canned tomatoes—on top of the duck legs to firmly compress them against each other. Place in the refrigerator overnight.

4. Remove the duck legs from the plastic container, pat them dry (they will have released quite a bit of liquid), and place them in a roasting pan or Dutch oven large enough to hold all 8 legs in a single layer. Scatter the rosemary sprigs and garlic cloves on top of the legs.

5. Preheat the oven to 225°F (110°C).

—continued—

COSCIA D'ANATRA CONFIT
(continued)

6. If using rendered duck fat, in a saucepan, heat the fat very slowly over low heat, just enough to liquify the fat. Allow to cool slightly. Pour the liquefied fat evenly over the duck legs. The fat should completely cover the duck legs. If it doesn't, simply add extra-virgin olive oil until the legs are covered. Cover the roasting pan with aluminum foil.

7. Place the duck legs on the middle rack of the oven and bake for 3½ to 4 hours, or until the duck legs become fork-tender and the meat can be easily pulled away from the bone.

8. Remove the pan from the oven, remove the aluminum foil covering from the pan, and allow the legs to cool to room temperature. Once cool, transfer the legs to a storage container, pour the cooking fat over the legs so they are completely covered, tightly cover the container, and store in the refrigerator. The legs can be stored this way for up to 2 weeks.

9. About 3 hours before serving, remove as many legs as needed from the storage container. Thoroughly wipe off all the fat and aromatics. Allow the legs to warm up to room temperature.

10. Heat 1 to 2 tablespoons of extra-virgin olive oil in a sauté pan large enough to accommodate the duck legs over medium-high heat. Carefully place the legs into the heated pan. (Be on the lookout for splattering fat!) Allow the legs to crisp up and take on some color on the first side, then turn and crisp up the other side. Serve on warmed plates.

Bonus Dish . . . Piatto di Recupero!

Confit duck legs are labor- and time-intensive, so be sure to make a large batch when you do tackle them. Simply bring the legs back up to room temperature, remove them from the fat, wipe off any excess fat, and you're ready to go with a reboot dish.

Though you could simply serve the duck legs the same way as initially intended, I like to mix things up. Shred the duck meat and blend it into a simple tomato sauce. Cook some fettucine, pappardelle, or maltagliati pasta and marry with the duck sauce. Eccolo! A gutsy, rib-sticking pasta dish for dinner in no time at all.

Make It a Meal: In French bistros, duck leg confit is traditionally served as an appetizer as presented here, but I also like this indulgent preparation as a main course with a side of creamy Tuscan white beans (page 191).

Wine Pairing: Fontodi Chianti Classico Gran Selezione DOCG "Vigna del Sorbo" 2018. One of Chianti's premier wines year in and year out, "Vigna del Sorbo" has the structure, complexity, and long finish in the mouth to make it the perfect partner for this rich duck indulgence.

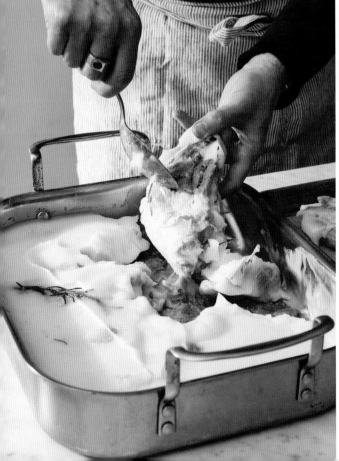

RAVIOLI AL LATTE CON PEPE NERO
Ravioli with Cream and Black Pepper

Eventually, Karly left the Buca. But she's never left Florence. And she's never left the kitchen. As a part-time food and beverage consultant and menu developer for a chain of boutique European hotels, she sets aside time to teach. Small groups of tourists, second homeowners, and even locals who know that "la ragazza americana" can cook Tuscan soul food with the best of them beat a steady path to her kitchen.

One day a few years back, Cyndy and I spent an afternoon with Karly, drinking good wine, laughing, and cooking through a greatest-hits list of Buca dell'Orafo classics. This simple pasta dish—rich with cream, cheese, and beautiful handmade tortelloni—is one of our favorites.

SERVES 4

Kosher or coarse sea salt

2½ cups (600 ml) heavy cream

1 pound (455 g) fresh cheese-filled ravioli or tortelloni (see A Note About Fresh Tortelloni and Ravioli, page 88)

½ cup (50 g) grated Parmigiano-Reggiano cheese, plus more for serving

Freshly ground black pepper

1. Bring a large pot of salted water to a boil.

2. Pour the heavy cream into a large sauté pan or saucepan over medium-high heat and bring it to a boil. Don't be afraid of letting the cream continue to boil a bit (but watch out—it will want to overflow your pan and you may need to stir and lower the heat every so often). You want the cream to reduce and slightly thicken, which usually takes 3 to 4 minutes. The cream won't "break" or curdle the way that milk might. Remove the pan from the heat.

3. Add the ravioli to the boiling water and cook until they've reached the "punto giusto" stage (see Some Thoughts on Pasta, page 36).

4. Return the saucepan with the cream back to the heat. Using a wire strainer, scoop the ravioli out of the pasta pot and toss them into the bubbling cream. Stir with a spoon to combine and "marry" the ravioli with the cream, taking time to let the two cook together. If the sauce and pasta mixture becomes too thick or dry, add some pasta cooking water to the pan and continue cooking until you get the right consistency. When the sauce coats the back of a spoon and, when swiped with a single finger, leaves a visible bare strip, you will have reached the desired consistency.

—continued—

RAVIOLI AL LATTE CON PEPE NERO
(continued)

5. Remove the pan from of the heat. Add the grated Parmigiano-Reggiano cheese and several generous grinds of black pepper to the pan and stir well to combine. Once again—and this is important!—if the mixture seems too thick or dry, which can happen after adding the cheese and as the mixture begins to cool a bit, add just a little bit more pasta cooking water to maintain the right consistency. Trust your senses on this.

6. Divide the pasta evenly among four warmed serving bowls, top each serving with a bit more grated cheese, and serve immediately.

A Note About Fresh Tortelloni and Ravioli

If you're lucky enough to live in or close to Florence, there's an artisanal pasta shop that cranks out fresh pasta of every shape and size imaginable. Tucked in among small storefronts in Florence's funky Via Palazzuolo neighborhood, Pasta Fresca Morioni is a throwback to another time and unfortunately, at least in the Tuscan region, a dying breed.

I generally prefer to make my own fresh pasta. Once you've gained some confidence working with pasta dough and cutting the basic noodle shapes, it's easy enough to create your own. But I have to admit, when it comes to stuffed pasta (ravioli, tortelloni, tortellini, agnolotti, etc.), you're treading into much more demanding territory, both in terms of the fillings and the shaping of the various pasta types. Enter Pasta Fresca Morioni.

I recommend you find a reliable source of stuffed fresh pasta and take advantage of the convenience. It's one less excuse for not trying that stuffed pasta recipe you've wanted to try. And, if you've found the right source, you will sacrifice nothing in the quality of your finished dish. Better supermarkets and specialty food stores around the U.S. carry fresh pasta from some very good producers. Check in the refrigerated foods section. Online resources like Eataly (you may be lucky enough to have a physical store nearby) are also great resources.

FIORI DI ZUCCA FRITTI
Fried Zucchini Blossoms

Another mainstay of Florentine trattoria menus—and a Buca dell'Orafo specialty—are fried zucchini blossoms. As an appetizer or a side dish, it's hard to beat these crispy-on-the-outside, light-on-the-inside, savory morsels of goodness. Fiori are widely available in fruit and vegetable markets throughout Tuscany, but admittedly more difficult to find in the U.S. Check local farmers' markets and specialty shops and grab them when they're in season.

Deep-frying at home can seem intimidating, but by observing a few general rules—as Karly has taught us—you'll be surprised at how good the results are.

Use enough oil to come halfway up the sides of your cooking vessel—never less and never more. Too little oil and you'll be pan frying; too much oil and you will run the risk of a spillover when cold ingredients hit the hot oil (and that is dangerous). I like the flavor profile and high smoke point of peanut oil for my deep-frying.

Make sure your oil reaches a perfect frying temperature of around 375°F (190°C). Any hotter and you risk burning the exterior of the food before it's cooked through; any lower and your food will turn out soggy and oily.

Finally, work in small batches and don't overcrowd your cooking vessel. Too much in at once and the cold food will lower the temperature of the oil dramatically, ruining your results. As you finish each small batch, place it on a paper towel–lined plate or sheet pan and put it in your oven (turned off) to keep it warm until you've finished all of your frying.

SERVES 4 AS AN ANTIPASTO OR CONTORNO

1 cup (140 g) all-purpose flour

12 ounces (360 ml) beer or sparkling mineral water

3 cups (720 ml) peanut or vegetable oil

16 fresh zucchini blossoms

Kosher or coarse sea salt

1. Place the flour in a medium bowl. Pour in just enough of the beer to cover the flour and whisk well to combine. Add more liquid, a little at a time as needed, to achieve a pancake batter–like consistency. The batter should be smooth with no lumps and should run off of the whisk in a slow stream. Cover the bowl tightly with plastic wrap and place the batter in your refrigerator to rest and cool for at least 1 hour.

2. In a large cast-iron or heavy-bottomed ceramic cooking vessel, pour in enough cooking oil to reach halfway up the sides of the vessel. Heat the oil over medium-high heat until it reaches 375°F (190°C) on a kitchen thermometer.

3. While the oil is heating, line a plate or baking sheet with paper towels. Remove the batter from the refrigerator and whisk well. Toss 4 or 5 zucchini blossoms into the bowl and "drag" each one through the batter to coat completely and evenly.

—continued—

FIORI DI ZUCCA FRITTI
(continued)

4. When the oil is at optimal frying temperature, pick up a battered blossom and let any excess batter fall back into the bowl. Place the battered blossom carefully into the oil and submerge it. Work in batches of no more than 4 or 5 blossoms at a time.

5. With a slotted spoon or wire mesh scoop, give the blossoms a gentle stir every so often and turn them over from time to time to encourage even frying and to keep the blossoms from sticking together. Fry until the blossoms are golden brown and the exteriors are visibly crispy, 2 to 3 minutes. Remove the blossoms from the oil, drain, and place them on a paper towel–lined plate or baking sheet. Generously season the blossoms with salt immediately. Place them in a turned-off oven while you fry the remaining blossoms.

6. When all of the blossoms have been fried and seasoned, place them on a serving tray and serve immediately.

Note: You can use this same technique to prepare other kinds of fried vegetables—zucchini sticks, broccoli florets, onion rings, sweet potato slices, or whatever you like. For these kinds of vegetables, a slightly thicker batter may give better results.

FERNANDO

Within a generation after Italy's unification in the late 1800s, waves of immigration to other parts of the world began as many Italians fled from poverty, regional prejudice, or political persecution. Hundreds of thousands of Italian immigrants landed at Ellis Island in New York. Canada, Australia, and Argentina were other popular destinations.

Fernando Marengo is a descendant of that Italian wave of immigration. In his family's case, Fernando's mother immigrated to central Argentina, where he was born and raised. Presented with the opportunity to play professional basketball in Italy and to reconnect with his Italian roots, Fernando moved to Italy some ten-plus years ago. He's played for various teams throughout Italy and established himself as a valued contributor. During a stint playing for Florence, he met his wife, Brigitta—a born-and-bred Gaiolese DOC. They fell in love, and now, this ever-smiling six-foot-two-inch-tall Italo-Argentinian is an official member of Gaiole's international transplant community.

When he's not on the basketball court, Fernando loves to cook. And like most Argentinians, he likes to cook meat—over a live fire.

On a lazy weekend afternoon in Tuscany, when there's no work to worry about and more time to dedicate to life's slow-lane pleasures, you might catch the scent of a whole suckling pig cooking slowly over coals or in a wood-burning oven until the meat is ready to fall off the bones and the pig's skin is caramelized and crackling. It's a six- to seven-hour affair.

Fernando has mastered the art of the suckling pig roast. He uses an old Argentinian technique that calls for the pig to be splayed open and secured to a metal cross, which is then placed close to a low-heat live fire and periodically basted with a brine/herb solution. Served with a spicy red chimichurri sauce and oven-roasted potatoes, this is a great celebration of simply prepared food that satisfies all the senses.

ARROSTO DI MAIALE
Slow-Roasted Pork Shoulder

For most home cooks, it would be a daunting task to replicate Fernando's whole suckling pig cooked "alla croce" near live fire. I think this roast pork recipe is a worthy substitute. When seasoned with plenty of Tuscan-style herbs and slowly cooked in a low oven, it makes a wonderful Sunday supper that would please the most demanding Tuscan family.

SERVES 6 TO 8

FOR THE PORK ROAST

1 (4- to 5-lb/1.8- to 2.25-kg) pork shoulder (sometimes labeled pork butt), bone-in if available, but boneless also works well

Kosher or coarse sea salt and freshly ground black pepper

4 to 5 tablespoons (40 to 45 g) fennel pollen

1 large yellow onion, quartered

2 large carrots, cut into 1-inch (2.5-cm) pieces

2 large celery stalks, cut into 1-inch (2.5-cm) pieces

3 garlic cloves, unpeeled

1 sprig fresh rosemary

1 sprig fresh thyme

2 sprigs fresh sage

½ bottle (375 ml) good-quality white wine, such as Pinot Grigio

Good-quality extra-virgin olive oil, for drizzling

1 lemon, cut in half

To cook the pork:

1. Preheat the oven to 275°F (135°C).

2. Generously season the pork on all sides with plenty of salt and pepper. Sprinkle the fennel pollen all over the pork and pat well to make sure it sticks to the surface of the meat.

3. Place the onion, carrots, celery, garlic, rosemary, thyme, sage, and white wine in a roasting pan just large enough to accommodate the meat. Place the pork shoulder on top of the vegetables and herbs. Cover the roasting pan tightly with aluminum foil. Place in the oven and roast until cooked through and tender, 6 to 7 hours. When you can insert a thin knife into the roast and feel little to no resistance, the roast should then be fork-tender and ready. If the meat still feels tough and resistant to the knife, additional cooking time is needed.

FOR THE CHIMICHURRI SAUCE

1 cup (240 ml) high-quality extra-virgin olive oil

¼ cup (60 ml) red wine vinegar

¼ cup (10 g) minced fresh Italian flat-leaf parsley

2 tablespoons (10 g) dried oregano

2 tablespoons (10 g) crushed red pepper flakes

2 tablespoons (15 g) sweet or smoked paprika

1 tablespoon (10 g) kosher salt

1 tablespoon (10 g) freshly ground black pepper

To make the chimichurri sauce:

4. While the pork is roasting, mix together the olive oil, red wine vinegar, parsley, oregano, red pepper flakes, paprika, salt, and pepper in a bowl. Let sit for at least 1 hour to allow the flavors to meld. The chimichurri can be made well ahead of time and stored for up to 1 week in the refrigerator.

To finish the dish:

5. When the roast has finished cooking, remove it from the oven, place it on a cutting board, cover loosely with aluminum foil, and allow to rest for at least 15 and up to 30 minutes. Carve into slices or simply pull serving-size pieces apart from the whole shoulder. Arrange on a serving platter, spoon a generous amount of the pan drippings on top of the meat, and finish with a drizzle of olive oil and a squeeze of fresh lemon. Serve with the spicy red chimichurri sauce on the side.

Make It a Meal: Roast pork lends itself well to any number of vegetable side dishes. We love it with roasted potatoes (page 201) and sautéed broccoli rabe (page 242).

Wine Pairing: I Sodi "Soprasassi" IGT Toscana 2020. Our Argentinian friend has an adventurous palate and he likes to explore outside-the-box wines like this 100 percent Canaiolo produced right in the heart of Gaiole.

ANDREA

Every Thursday, a local fish monger arrives in the main parking lot on the edge of town. It's a mobile operation with a dazzling array of fresh Mediterranean fish and shellfish, and it's a very popular weekly shopping destination for locals craving a break from Chianti's meat-heavy diet. If you arrive early, your chances of securing a sack of "vongole veraci" are pretty good. These small, sweet clams are the preferred choice of in-the-know cooks for one of coastal Italy's most beloved dishes—spaghetti alle vongole.

It's another one of those deceptively simple dishes that can leave you disappointed if it's not executed with the attention to detail and confidence of an experienced hand. Enter our friend Andrea Povia.

Andrea is another Southern Italian transplant. In a town very much dominated by Tuscan flavors and traditions, Andrea's small bistro just a few steps from Gaiole's main piazza is a completely different animal. It's a place where—in Andrea's words—"la Puglia incontra la Toscana" (Apulia meets Tuscany). Locals and tourists alike are drawn to this jewel box of a restaurant by Andrea's deft hand with Pugliese seafood specialties.

On Thursdays, people come for the spaghetti alle vongole prepared with clams procured that day from the visiting fish monger.

SPAGHETTI ALLE VONGOLE
Spaghetti with Clams, White Wine, and Garlic

As with most Italian classics, only a few ingredients combine to produce a final result that is greater than the simple sum of its individual parts—clams, white wine, olive oil, pepperoncino, and a last-minute shower of fresh flat-leaf parsley. As usual, the devil is in the details.

As an accommodation to my own personal preference, I've modified Andrea's method slightly by suggesting that most of the clams be removed from their shells just before they're fully cooked and then finished in the all-important "marrying" phase of the sauce and the pasta. That way, it's a far less labor-intensive eating experience. A few clams are left in their shells—just to convey the message that this is a real-deal fresh shellfish pasta dish. I also substitute littleneck clams, which are much more readily available in the U.S., for the vongole veraci.

Most mistakes with this dish are made in the final stage—the emulsifying, mixing, and combining of the pasta and sauce. You don't want soup, but you also don't want a dry, sticky mass. Use your senses and judgment. If it seems too dry, add a bit more pasta water. If it seems too wet, place the pan back on the heat to evaporate some of the mixture. Trust yourself!

I recommend a side of thick grilled slices of hearty country bread generously doused with best-quality extra-virgin olive oil and sprinkled with sea salt. You'll want to sop up every drop of clam sauce in the bottom of your bowl.

Italians will scold you if you put cheese on top of this pasta. But I say do as you please.

SERVES 4

Kosher or coarse sea salt

½ cup (120 ml) high-quality extra-virgin olive oil, plus more as needed

1 garlic clove, cut in half

1 jalapeño, Scotch bonnet, or similar fresh chile pepper to bring the heat (or crushed red pepper flakes), minced

4 dozen littleneck clams (you want clams on the smaller side; cherrystones, for example, would not work), well rinsed

1 cup (240 ml) dry white wine (use something that you'd be happy to drink)

–continued–

1. Bring a large pot of salted water to a boil.

2. In a large, deep sauté pan or heavy casserole cooking pot, heat the olive oil over medium-low heat. Add the garlic and turn the heat to low to allow the flavor of the garlic to slowly infuse the oil without burning.

3. Add the fresh chile pepper to the pan. Add the clams, pour in the white wine, and raise the heat to medium-high. When the liquid begins to boil and steam, cover the pan tightly.

4. Check on the clams every minute or so. As soon as most of the clams have opened, take the pan off of the heat. Scoop out the clams, drain them well to ensure that most of their cooking juices remain in the pan, and place them in a bowl to cool slightly. Discard any unopened clams; they may not be fit for consumption.

5. Set aside a dozen of the clams in their shells. Remove the rest of the clams from their shells and place them in a small bowl.

—continued—

1 pound (455 g) spaghetti or linguine

Chopped fresh flat-leaf parsley

Grilled bread, for serving

6. Put the spaghetti into the boiling salted water, giving it a stir after a minute or so to make sure nothing has stuck to the bottom of the pot. Cook until just al dente (see Some Thoughts on Pasta, page 36).

7. As the pasta is cooking, reheat the pan with the olive oil/wine/clam juice mixture over medium heat. Add a half ladle or so of the pasta cooking water to the pan and bring to a boil to emulsify everything into a well-combined sauce.

8. When the pasta has reached the al dente point, use a pair of tongs to remove it from the pot and transfer it to the sauté pan. Don't worry too much about draining the pasta well, as the additional pasta cooking water will actually help you finish and "marry" the dish. Put all the shelled clams into the pan and stir the clams and pasta well to combine them with the sauce, shaking the pan as you do so. If the mixture becomes too dry, add a little more pasta water.

9. When everything has been nicely combined and emulsified, take the pan off of the heat, drizzle with olive oil, and sprinkle with chopped parsley. Stir well one last time to incorporate the oil and parsley and, if necessary, add a bit more pasta water to keep everything just wet enough.

10. Portion into warmed bowls, top each bowl with a few of the clams in their shells, and serve immediately with grilled bread.

Make It a Meal: This is a dish that, for me, is best enjoyed in the summertime as a main course. Begin with a bright fennel and blood orange salad (page 245) to jump-start your appetite.

Wine Pairing: Bucci Verdicchio Classico Superiore dei Castelli di Jesi DOC 2022. We could stay in Tuscany with a vermentino or a vernaccia for this dish, but I love this wine from one of the Marche region's flagship producers.

PARMIGIANA ALLA NAPOLETANA
Eggplant Parmigiana Neapolitan-Style

In the height of the summer season, local vegetable gardens are overflowing with eggplant. There are so many ways to prepare it—simply grilled with olive oil; sautéed with a hint of tomato and basil; as the base of a Sicilian-style caponata; or my favorite, layered into a sumptuous parmigiana alla napoletana.

Andrea prepares his in the traditional style with layers of fresh-made tomato sauce, fried eggplant, fior di latte cheese, grated Parmigiano-Reggiano, and basil. Sometimes he'll sneak in some prosciutto.

It's a dish that may be even better prepared the day before, allowed to rest with the flavors melding together overnight, and reheated the next day.

There are three parts to this recipe: making the fresh tomato sauce; cutting, salting, and frying the eggplant; and the final assembly of the dish. It can seem overwhelming, but they are all simple, straightforward kitchen skills. Time consuming—yes; difficult—no. The end result is worth it.

SERVES 4 TO 6

FOR THE BASIC TOMATO SAUCE

¼ cup (60 ml) high-quality extra-virgin olive oil

2 or 3 garlic cloves, minced

2 (28-oz/784-g) cans high-quality whole San Marzano tomatoes, hand crushed with their juices

Kosher or coarse sea salt and freshly ground black pepper

—continued—

To make the tomato sauce:

1. Heat the olive oil over low heat in a sauté pan large enough to accommodate the tomatoes. Toss in the garlic and let it slowly cook until it takes on a light strawlike color. Don't let the garlic burn—it will bring a bitter flavor to your sauce.

2. Add the tomatoes, season generously with salt and pepper to taste, and stir to thoroughly combine the ingredients.

3. Raise the heat to medium-high and bring the tomatoes to a moderate boil. Cook for about 5 minutes, stirring frequently, until the tomatoes and oil begin to come together as one.

4. Lower the heat and continue to cook at a slow, steady simmer; 20 to 25 minutes is generally enough to bring the sauce to the right consistency. Taste for seasoning and add more salt and pepper if needed. If the sauce seems too thick at any point during cooking, add a little bit of water to the pan to bring it back to the desired consistency.

5. The sauce can be prepared well in advance, cooled, transferred to a sealable plastic container, and stored in the refrigerator for up to 1 week. Not only is this sauce a key ingredient in parmigiana alla napoletana, but it is also used in many other recipes in this book. Makes about 1½ quarts (1.4 L).

—continued—

PARMIGIANA ALLA NAPOLETANA
(continued)

FOR THE EGGPLANT

6 to 8 medium eggplants
(3.75 lb/1.7 kg)

Kosher or coarse sea salt

High-quality extra-virgin olive oil

2 cups (280 g) toasted bread crumbs
(optional)

1 pound (455 g) fresh cow's milk
mozzarella

2 cups (200 g) freshly grated
Parmigiano-Reggiano cheese

1 cup (20 g) fresh basil leaves

Freshly ground black pepper

To prepare the eggplant:

6. Line a baking sheet with paper towels.

7. Cut off the tips of the eggplants to create a flat surface at each end. Stand a piece on one of its flat ends and, using a sharp kitchen knife, thinly cut off the skin on two opposite "sides," creating two more flat surfaces on the eggplant. Discard the pieces of skin.

8. Cut each eggplant lengthwise into ¼-inch (6-mm) thick slices, starting from one of the flat sides and working toward the other.

9. Place a layer of eggplant slices on the paper towel–lined baking sheet and sprinkle them generously with salt on both sides. Cover with another layer of paper towels, place more slices on top, sprinkle both sides with salt, and cover again with another layer of paper towels. Repeat until all the eggplant slices have been layered and salted. Cover the layered baking sheet with another baking sheet and place several heavy cans (could be tomatoes, could be canned beans—anything heavy) on top to press down on the eggplant. This pre-salting technique will extract a lot of the eggplant's bitter juice and also make frying easier. Allow the eggplant to sit for 1 hour.

10. Remove the weighted tray and the paper towels (which should have absorbed quite a bit of liquid) from the eggplant layers. Pat dry with fresh paper towels and set the eggplant slices aside. Line a clean baking sheet with paper towels.

11. Pour about 2 inches (5 cm) of olive oil into a large sauté or frying pan over medium-high heat. You need the oil to be hot enough to create an immediate sizzle when an eggplant slice hits the oil, but not so hot that it will simply burn without cooking through. If the oil is too cold, the eggplant will absorb too much oil and will not cook properly.

12. Place 4 or 5 slices (depending on the size of your pan; do not overcrowd the pan or you will not achieve the desired result) of eggplant into the hot oil and fry on one side until a golden-brown caramelization begins. Flip each slice over and continue cooking. Be careful; the second side will cook much faster than the first. This is a time to be vigilant. Remove the fried slices and place them on the paper towel–lined baking sheet. Repeat the process until all the eggplant has been fried.

Oil and Eggplant If your oil is at the right temperature, you should only need to add more to the pan once or twice during the cooking process. Yes, the eggplant will absorb and retain some oil. But the amount of retained oil should not be excessive and will contribute to the richness of the finished dish. As you become more familiar with cooking eggplant in this way, you'll notice that initially the slices will absorb a lot of oil and then, as they cook, will release much of that oil back into the pan. Again—as I advise so many times in this book— use your judgment and your common sense. Adjust the heat up or down as necessary during frying. Add only as much additional olive oil as necessary to the pan. Trust your instincts!

To assemble the dish:

13. In a ceramic baking dish large enough to accommodate four or five layers of the assembled dish, start by spreading a moderate amount of the tomato sauce on the bottom of the baking dish.

14. Place a layer of eggplant slices over the tomato sauce, keeping them close together and covering the entire surface of the dish. If necessary, cut some of the eggplant slices to fit or slightly overlap a few slices.

15. If using toasted bread crumbs, sprinkle them on. They add an additional texture to the dish and can also absorb and balance out any excess moisture from the mozzarella.

16. Top the bread crumbs with a generous scattering of hand-torn pieces of mozzarella, and sprinkle generously with the grated Parmigiano-Reggiano and torn basil leaves. Top with dollops of the tomato sauce. Don't overdo the sauce; the key to success with this dish is balance between the ingredients.

17. Repeat the layering process until you've created four or five layers depending on the size of your baking dish. The final layer should consist only of eggplant slices, a moderate amount of tomato sauce, and an extra-generous shower of Parmigiano-Reggiano. Finish with a drizzle of olive oil over the top.

18. Cover the fully assembled dish with aluminum foil and allow to rest for at least 1 hour before baking or refrigerate overnight and proceed with baking the next day.

—continued—

PARMIGIANA ALLA NAPOLETANA
(continued)

To bake the dish:

19. Preheat the oven to 400°F (200°C).

20. Uncover the baking dish and place it on the middle rack of the oven. Bake for 25 to 35 minutes, until heated through, bubbling, and browned on top. Check the dish's progress every once in a while. It's best to leave the dish uncovered to promote evaporation of excess moisture that can make the final result too soggy. But, if the eggplant appears to be browning too quickly on top, either lower the heat or cover the eggplant loosely with aluminum foil for part of the remaining baking time.

21. Remove the eggplant from the oven and allow to rest for 20 minutes or so. If you cut into it immediately after baking, it will not have had a chance to "set" and will likely be runny and difficult to portion out.

22. Cut the rested eggplant into individual servings, place each on a warmed plate, and serve immediately with an additional sprinkling of Parmigiano-Reggiano and a drizzle of olive oil on top.

Bonus Dish . . . Piatto di Recupero!
The tomato sauce is very versatile as a base for many different pasta sauces or as an addition to sautéed vegetables like zucchini or green beans. As mentioned above, the sauce will keep in a sealed plastic container in your refrigerator for up to 1 week. We always have some on hand for a simple spur-of-the-moment pasta dinner. Other recipes in this book that use the Basic Tomato Sauce include polpettine (page 119), spaghetti napoli (page 139), and penne al sugo di salsiccia (page 170), among others.

Make It a Meal: I love parmigiana as a gutsy starter followed by a lighter main course like branzino al forno (page 179).

Wine Pairing: Castello di Brolio Chianti Classico DOCG 2020. Simple, straightforward, and delicious, this offering from the "birthplace" of Chianti is pure "Gaiole in a bottle."

SUE

One of Rome's most iconic streets is Via Margutta, not too far from the Spanish Steps and the city's chic shopping district. It's probably best known for being the longtime address of the Italian filmmaker Federico Fellini. It's a quiet street—hard to believe that one block over is the chaotic Via del Babuino where a single misstep off of the narrow sidewalk can land you in a collision with a speeding Vespa or worse. The street is lined with small shops. One of our favorites is at Number 55.

Ironically, there is no sign at Number 55 indicating either the name of the shop or what lies within. Ironic, indeed, because the longtime owner and artisan, Sandro, deals exclusively in handmade marble signs, each personally inscribed with a witty, and usually irreverent, phrase. One example in Roman dialect: "È mejo puzza' de vino che d'acquasanta" (Better to stink of wine than holy water). You get the idea.

One day during a spur-of-the-moment trip to the Eternal City, we popped in and discovered one of Sandro's simpler works. It read simply "CIAO Y'ALL." We immediately knew where this particular sign needed to go.

Our dear friend Sue Palmer is a Texas transplant who has made Gaiole her full-time residence for more than fifteen years. It would not be exaggeration to call Sue a true renaissance woman. She's a successful entrepreneur, having founded and operated her own fuel distributorship and chain of convenience stores. She was a Texas state representative and active in Texas politics and public affairs for many years. Even in retirement she's in constant motion, volunteering time toward local affairs and helping other ex-pats navigate Italy's bureaucratic house of mirrors. In her "downtime" she's likely hiking local trails with her dog, Lucio, or organizing a long Sunday lunch for friends at her home—one of her favorite things to do.

A Sunday lunch at Sue's is always fun and interesting: a mix of ex-pat residents and locals, maybe some visiting friends or family, and a lot of good wine and laughter. The food can be surprising. A "themed" meal is sometimes the order of the day, and for a local it can seem pretty exotic. There've been Mexican, Asian, and Greek meals, and sometimes Tex-Mex. There is something oddly satisfying about a bowl of spicy green Texas chili on a crisp fall afternoon in Chianti. I know it's not remotely Tuscan, but it's part of our local experience. And damn, it's good!!

SUE'S GREEN TEXAS CHILI

One of the biggest challenges of a themed lunch in Chianti is finding "exotic" ingredients. Not a lot of demand for tomatillos in Gaiole. Somehow, Sue manages to track down what she needs. This will not, ironically, be a problem for readers in the U.S. Maybe you will struggle to find guanciale for a carbonara, but everything for this recipe should be readily available to you.

Many traditional recipes for Texas green chili call for beef. This version substitutes pork shoulder, adding a slightly Tuscan take on this Southwest American classic.

SERVES 6 TO 8

1 pound (455 g) assorted whole fresh chile peppers (poblano, Anaheim, jalapeño)

½ cup (120 ml) high-quality extra-virgin olive oil

2 pounds (910 g) pork shoulder (sometimes called butt), cut into cubes

Kosher or coarse sea salt and freshly ground black pepper

3 garlic cloves, minced

2 yellow or white onions, chopped

4 cups (960 ml) chicken stock or broth

8 ounces (230 g) tomatillos, skin removed and halved

1 tablespoon (10 g) ground cumin

1 tablespoon (10 g) dried oregano

Sour cream

½ cup (10 g) chopped fresh cilantro

1. Preheat the oven to 300°F (150°C).

2. Place the chile peppers on a baking sheet and roast them, turning them occasionally, until blistered and charred, 25 to 30 minutes. Place them in a bowl and cover tightly with plastic wrap so they steam.

3. When the peppers are cool enough to handle, remove the stems. Roughly cut into chunks.

4. In a large pot (ideally a cast-iron enamel Dutch oven or casserole), heat the olive oil over medium-high heat. Season the pork cubes generously with salt and pepper and brown them well all over. Don't crowd the pork cubes or they will steam rather than sear and caramelize. If necessary, brown them in a few batches, setting aside the browned cubes on a plate while you finish the rest.

5. Once all the meat has been browned, lower the heat a bit and toss the garlic and onions into the pot. Cook slowly, stirring occasionally with a wooden spoon, until slightly softened and the onions are translucent.

6. Add enough chicken stock to the onion and garlic mixture to cover the bottom of the pot. Bring to a boil, scrape up the brown bits and caramelization from the bottom of the pot, and incorporate into the liquid. Add the meat back to the pot, then add the tomatillos, cumin, and oregano, and stir well to combine. Keep the chopped roasted chile peppers in reserve to be added to the mixture at a later time (see step 7). Add enough additional chicken stock to cover the meat and vegetable mixture.

7. Bring the liquid back to a boil, then lower the heat to a simmer. At this point, you could continue to slowly simmer the contents of the pot on the stove, checking from time to time to make sure that not too much liquid has evaporated, until the meat is fork-tender, about 3 hours. Alternatively, you could cover the pot and place it in a 300°F (150°C) oven for 3 to 4 hours, until the meat is fork-tender. When about 1 hour of cooking time remains, add the chopped roasted chile peppers to the pot, stir to combine, and continue cooking. Be patient to reach the consistency you're after.

8. Taste for seasoning and, if necessary, add salt and pepper. Serve the finished chili in warmed serving bowls with the sour cream and fresh chopped cilantro on the side.

Beer Pairing: Birra BVS Valdarno Pale Ale Toscana. I love my wine, but chili demands a beer! This artisanal pale ale is produced about 30 minutes northeast of Gaiole in Montevarchi. If it's difficult to find in the U.S., you could go with a readily available Italian classic like Birra Moretti as a substitute.

ANTONIETTA

Every year in late October, Cyndy and I—assisted by a loyal group of local friends—harvest our fifty olive trees. Within a couple of days, our efforts are rewarded with a flow of "olio nuovo" (new oil) so green it doesn't seem real. Unfiltered and free from any kind of industrial processing, this early-harvest olive oil has a distinct peppery bite and pleasant pungency. Olive oil like this rarely reaches the U.S.

Within hours of the oil's pressing, we're all gathered together for the season's first bruschette, grilled slices of hearty Tuscan bread drowned in copious amounts of new oil and sprinkled with sea salt. It's Tuscan simplicity as its best.

This generations-old food ritual—something that Tuscans anticipate each year with palpable excitement—is just one example of how food brings people together here. It's not just the quality of Tuscan cooking and ingredients, which is extraordinarily high, that draws me to this food. It's also the importance that people from all walks of life place on eating well and spending time at the table with friends and family.

Two of our most loyal harvest team members are Antonietta and her husband, Donato, both of whom originally hail from Campania, the Southern Italian region encompassing the city of Naples and the Amalfi Coast. Antonietta is a great cook and, with some coaxing, can usually be convinced to make some Campanian contributions to our annual "new oil" harvest dinner. Here are three of my favorites.

ORECCHIETTE CON SALSICCIA E CIME DI RAPE

Orecchiette with Sausage and Broccoli Rabe

This is a classic Campanian dish—orecchiette (literally "little ears") made with nothing more than a mix of double zero and semolina flours and water, dressed with a simple sauce of Italian sausage and broccoli rabe. The richness of the sausage is counterbalanced by the bracing bitterness of the greens and it's all brought together by the satisfying dense chewiness of the pasta. I like to take one liberty of my own with Antonietta's recipe by mixing a teaspoon of honey into the sauce toward the end of cooking, which brings a bit of balance to the dish and takes the edge off of the bitter broccoli rabe.

SERVES 4

Kosher or coarse sea salt

2 medium bunches broccoli rabe

½ cup (120 ml) high-quality extra-virgin olive oil, plus more as needed

1 garlic clove, cut into 3 or 4 small pieces

1 small dried chile pepper, crushed, or ½ teaspoon (2 g) chopped preserved Calabrian chile pepper

Freshly ground black pepper

Honey (optional)

Lemon juice

4 or 5 Italian sausage links (about 1 lb/455 g), casings removed

1 pound (455 g) orecchiette

Parmigiano-Reggiano cheese

1. Bring a large pot (big enough to comfortably hold the broccoli rabe) of water to a boil. Meanwhile, prepare an ice bath in a large bowl by combining a generous amount of ice with cold water. When the water in the pot has reached a rolling boil, generously season it with salt and add the broccoli rabe. Cook for about 3 minutes, just long enough to soften the greens a bit. Remove the greens from the boiling water and immediately submerge them in the ice bath to stop the cooking and hold their bright color. Set aside 2 cups (480 ml) of the cooking water.

2. When the broccoli rabe has completely cooled, remove it from the ice bath, squeeze it well to remove most of the water, and set it aside on a cutting board. Roughly chop into bite-size pieces.

3. Heat the olive oil in a skillet over medium-high heat. Add the garlic, turn the heat down to medium-low, and allow it to simmer in the oil until it just starts to turn golden.

4. Add the crushed chile pepper, stir briefly, and then add the broccoli rabe. If needed, add a bit more olive oil to the pan to coat the broccoli rabe well and provide it with a nice sheen. Add salt and pepper to taste. Stir everything together well to combine. Turn the heat up a bit and sauté the broccoli rabe for 2 to 3 minutes.

—continued—

ORECCHIETTE CON SALSICCIA E CIME DI RAPE *(continued)*

5. Add just enough of the reserved broccoli rabe cooking water to cover the bottom of the pan. Lower the heat to maintain a bare simmer and allow the greens to slowly braise for 5 to 7 minutes with the pan covered but the lid slightly ajar. Turn off the heat and set the pan aside. Taste the broccoli rabe for seasoning, adding more salt and pepper if needed, and a bit of honey, if you'd like, to balance the bitterness of the greens. A squirt of lemon juice will also brighten the finished greens.

6. While the broccoli rabe is braising, cook the sausage in a separate pan. Add just enough olive oil to the pan to keep the sausage from sticking when it starts to cook. Add the sausage, crumbling it into small pieces as it goes into the pan, and cook over medium-high heat, stirring and breaking up the sausage into smaller pieces, until the sausage is completely browned, 5 to 7 minutes. Add some of the reserved broccoli rabe cooking water to the pan, turn the heat up to high, and deglaze the contents of the pan, scraping up the browned bits from the bottom of the pan until they are incorporated into the sausage. Turn off the heat and set aside.

7. Bring a large pot of salted water to a boil over high heat.

8. Add the orecchiette to the boiling water, stir, and cook until the pasta reaches al dente (see Some Thoughts on Pasta, page 36).

9. While the orecchiette are cooking, add the sausage to the broccoli rabe mixture, stir well to combine, and reheat slowly over medium-low heat. Add a bit more of the reserved broccoli rabe cooking liquid to the pan to help create a sauce-like consistency.

10. Using a slotted spoon or spider, transfer the al dente orecchiette to the pan with the broccoli rabe and sausage mixture. Add a generous spoonful or two of the pasta cooking water, stir well to combine, and continue cooking over low heat to "marry" the orecchiette with the sauce and emulsify. Turn off the heat, add a generous handful of Parmigiano-Reggiano and a drizzle of olive oil, and combine everything well one last time. Serve immediately in warmed pasta bowls.

Note: The broccoli rabe and sausage mixture can be made up to a day in advance, stored in the refrigerator, and then reheated when you're ready to cook the pasta.

Make It a Meal: What more could you ask for? Antonietta serves her insalata caprese (page 122) as an antipasto, followed by these orecchiette as a primo, and rounds things out with her polpettine (page 119) as a secondo.

Wine Pairing: Casa di Bricciano Chianti Classico DOCG 2019. This Chianti from a small family-run vineyard in nearby Barbischio is the perfect accompaniment to this Campanian classic.

POLPETTINE
Meatballs

What makes a great meatball? This can be a subject of much debate. Beef, pork, veal, or some combination? Fried, baked, or braised? Baseball-size or mini? For me it comes down to two things: taste and texture. I want great umami-bomb flavor balanced by a melt-in-the-mouth consistency. Antonietta's hit the mark.

Here's my take on Antonietta's polpettine. The key is bread—lots of it. The cheaper and simpler the bread, the better. A supermarket white loaf is ideal. A large proportion, I'd say 30 percent of your meatball mix, should consist of milk-soaked bread "mush." That's what will give you tender meatballs. Don't skimp on this ingredient.

MAKES 15 TO 20 MEATBALLS, ABOUT 2 INCHES (5 CM) IN DIAMETER

8 slices plain white sandwich bread, crust removed

1 cup (240 ml) whole milk

12 ounces (340 g) ground veal

12 ounces (340 g) 70% to 80% lean ground beef

1 cup (100 g) grated Parmigiano-Reggiano cheese

1 cup (40 g) finely minced Italian flat-leaf parsley, plus more for garnish

1 garlic clove, minced

1 large egg

¼ cup (60 g) sour cream or crème fraîche

Freshly ground black pepper

3 or 4 drops fish sauce or Worcestershire sauce

Kosher or coarse sea salt

1 batch Basic Tomato Sauce (page 105)

High-quality extra-virgin olive oil

Orange zest (optional)

1. Break up the white bread slices by hand into small pieces, place them in a bowl, and cover with just enough of the milk to completely submerge them. Let soak for 5 to 10 minutes. Squeeze the bread mixture into a soft mush. Drain off any excess milk in the bowl.

2. Put the ground meats, Parmigiano-Reggiano cheese, parsley, garlic, egg, and sour cream into a large bowl. Add the soaked bread mixture, several generous grinds of fresh pepper, and the fish sauce and mix very thoroughly with your hands. Cover the bowl with plastic wrap and refrigerate for at least 1 hour or up to 4 hours. This cold resting period will allow the mixture to hydrate, meld together, and firm up for easier handling and shaping.

3. Line a baking sheet with parchment paper.

4. Add three or four generous pinches of salt to the bowl and mix well to combine. Form the mixture into individual meatballs by taking some of the meat mixture with your fingers, rolling it between your palms, and continuing to roll and compact until you have a fairly smooth ball. The size depends on your preference, but a diameter of about 2 inches (5 cm) is best for cooking. It helps to wet your hands periodically when forming the balls. Set the formed meatballs aside on the parchment-lined baking sheet.

—continued—

POLPETTINE
(continued)

5. In a wide shallow pan, heat the tomato sauce over medium-high heat until it begins to bubble. Place the meatballs into the sauce, being careful to leave enough space between them so you'll be able to roll them around as the cooking progresses. If you can't fit them all in comfortably in a single layer, cook them in batches.

6. Braise the meatballs in the sauce at a low, steady simmer with the cover slightly ajar for 7 to 8 minutes. Delicately turn each meatball over—this is most easily accomplished with a large soup spoon. The meatballs will be cooked through in 20 to 25 minutes of total cooking time. If cooking in batches, remove the cooked meatballs, place them on a platter, and repeat the cooking process until all the meatballs are finished. Return all the cooked meatballs to the pan, cover, and allow to rest for at least 20 minutes before serving. When ready to serve, simply reheat.

7. Serve the meatballs family-style on a large warmed platter. Top with some of the tomato sauce, a drizzle of extra-virgin olive, and a sprinkling of chopped parsley. To add a bit of freshness to the finished dish, I sometimes like to grate a small amount of orange zest (not too much—it's a powerful ingredient) on top, but this is strictly optional and dependent on your personal taste.

Bonus Dish . . . *Piatto di Recupero!*
Although unlikely, you may have both leftover meatballs and sauce after this meal. They can easily become the base for a great pasta dish in the following days. Simply break up a few of the meatballs into the sauce and reheat it. Even if all that's left over is the sauce itself, there will still be meatball "remnants" in the sauce, sufficient to create a hearty condiment for some pasta. I like to serve this sauce with penne and a shower of Parmigiano-Reggiano cheese. You'll have dinner on the table in less than 20 minutes.

Wine Pairing: Casa di Bricciano "Il Ritrovo" IGT Toscano 2016. Another selection from family-run Bricciano, this Super Tuscan's rich fruit and earthiness go well with these meatballs.

INSALATA CAPRESE
Fresh Tomato, Mozzarella, and Basil Salad

Nothing is more Campanian than an insalata caprese (the term *caprese* translates as "from Capri," the famous island not far off the Amalfi Coast). Though you'll find this simple antipasto in trattorias and restaurants throughout Italy, its origins and its best renditions are in Campania.

One summer, at the height of tomato season, Antonietta prepared us a simple insalata caprese with garden-fresh tomatoes, basil, and DOP buffalo mozzarella from Campania that a cousin had brought up to Chianti a few days earlier. It was another reminder of how the simplest dishes—this one requiring no cooking at all—can startle you with flavor when built upon the best, freshest ingredients available.

Imported DOP buffalo mozzarella is generally available at specialty cheese shops, Italian markets, or through importers like Eataly. But if you can't find it, simple cow's milk mozzarella (fiori di latte) is a fine substitute and typically easier to find. There are many quality domestic producers.

If it's wintertime and tomatoes are out of season, substitute roasted red peppers. They're a delicious alternative and certainly better than mass-produced greenhouse tomatoes.

SERVES 4 AS AN ANTIPASTO

4 large garden-fresh tomatoes at their peak of ripeness (or substitute roasted red peppers)

4 balls fresh buffalo or cow's milk mozzarella

12 to 14 fresh basil leaves

Kosher or coarse sea salt and freshly ground black pepper

High-quality extra-virgin olive oil

1. Cut the tomatoes into generous slices, 4 or 5 slices per tomato depending on the size. Cut the mozzarella into similar-size slices.

2. On each of four salad plates, arrange 4 or 5 slices of tomato and 4 or 5 slices of mozzarella, layering and alternating each ingredient.

3. Tear the basil leaves into small pieces by hand and scatter over each plate.

4. Season generously with salt and pepper. Drizzle very generously with olive oil. Serve immediately. This is a dish best prepared and eaten at the moment.

SERGIO

Romans are proud and stubborn people. When they emphatically state that theirs is the most beautiful and vibrant city, not just in Italy but in the world, you know that there's no debating that "fact." They are no less passionate about their food.

My friend Sergio is as Roman as it gets. Born and raised in the city and a lifelong resident, he is my authority on all things Roman, be it soccer, politics, or authentic Roman cuisine.

Not long after meeting him and his wife, Antonella, we invited them to our home for dinner. Now you must understand, all Italians have an opinion on food and all share one in common: Americans can't possibly cook good Italian food. So expectations were low and suspicions high when Sergio came to dinner.

To make matters worse, I had decided to prepare a pasta course of rigatoni all'amatriciana—one of Rome's most famous and hallowed dishes. Romans don't believe that Italians from other regions can make it properly, let alone an American transplant from Boston. But on I pushed, confident in my mastery of the dish.

As Sergio hovered behind me at the stove, I could sense he felt something was terribly wrong. But from my perspective, all was going well. My amatriciana sauce was coming together toward a perfect consistency, and I'd stopped the cooking of the rigatoni at that sweet spot just short of al dente. That would leave me enough additional cooking time to perfectly "marry" the rigatoni with the sauce, a technique that is—as I've emphatically stated in previous recipes herein—unfortunately little understood and even less observed in U.S. kitchens.

I finished the dish and we all sat down to eat. As far as I was concerned, I'd hit the ball out of the park. The dish was delicious. But I nervously awaited judgment from my Roman friend.

"John . . . Complimenti!! This is a very, very good pasta dish."

"Grazie, Sergio," I replied. "You have no idea how much that means to me."

"However—John—I must tell you. This is not amatriciana."

"What do you mean? Of course it's amatriciana. I made this especially for you."

"John—you cannot have an amatriciana without guanciale. You used pancetta. For me—for any native Roman—you must use guanciale. To use pancetta is to disrespect this important dish."

Huh. Who knew that the substitution of cured pork belly (pancetta) for cured pork cheek (guanciale) would disqualify a pasta dish from regional authentication. But therein lies a lesson: a Roman friend will love you unconditionally, but he will also call you out on your culinary shortcomings without pulling any punches.

Here are Sergio's ways with two of Rome's most beloved dishes.

RIGATONI ALL'AMATRICIANA
Rigatoni Amatriciana-Style

I learned something important from my attempt at making what I thought was an amatriciana for Sergio. Guanciale and pancetta are completely different (and noninterchangeable) pork ingredients. Guanciale is from the jowl or cheek of the pig and it has a distinct flavor profile. Gamier and fattier than pancetta, it's a great contrast to the sweet tomatoes and onions in an amatriciana sauce. Pancetta has its place in the Italian pantry and in many dishes. But if you want to recreate the Roman holy trinity of pasta dishes—amatriciana, carbonara, and la gricia—find yourself some guanciale.

SERVES 4

6 to 8 thick-cut slices guanciale (may substitute pancetta, but don't call it amatriciana!)

½ cup (120 ml) high-quality extra-virgin olive oil, plus more as needed

1 medium red onion, cut into ¼-inch (6-mm) pieces

1 (28-oz/784-g) can high-quality whole San Marzano tomatoes, hand crushed with their juices

Kosher or coarse sea salt and freshly ground black pepper

½ teaspoon (2 g) chopped preserved Calabrian chile pepper (optional)

1 pound (455 g) rigatoni

Pecorino romano or Parmigiano-Reggiano cheese

1. Bring a large pot of water to a boil over high heat.

2. Cut the guanciale into 1-inch (2.5-cm) long "baton" strips. Place in a large sauté pan over medium-low heat and cook for 2 to 3 minutes, until the guanciale just begins to take on some color. You do not want crispy guanciale; it should retain a relatively soft, meaty texture. Go slow and take your time. Transfer the sautéed guanciale to a plate and set aside.

3. Drain off all but about 2 tablespoons (30 ml) of the guanciale fat from the pan. Add the olive oil and onion and sauté until just translucent. Add the tomatoes, salt and pepper to taste, and the Calabrian chile pepper (if using) and mix well to incorporate. Add back the cooked guanciale strips. Bring to a vigorous boil over medium-high heat, then lower the heat to maintain a simmer and cook for 20 to 25 minutes. If at any time during the cooking the sauce seems to be thickening too much (approaching the consistency of a paste as opposed to a hearty sauce), add a bit of water to the pan to maintain the proper consistency. Taste for seasoning and add more salt or pepper, if needed. Turn off the heat and set aside.

4. Add a generous amount of salt to the pot of boiling water. Add the rigatoni and cook until just shy of al dente (see Some Thoughts on Pasta, page 36).

5. While the rigatoni is cooking, transfer some of the finished amatriciana sauce from the pan to a storage container, leaving enough sauce in the pan to adequately mix with the pasta. (You can always add more of the sauce to the pan later, if needed. Remember, you want to dress your pasta like a salad; it should not be swimming in sauce.)

—continued—

RIGATONI ALL'AMATRICIANA
(continued)

6. Using a slotted spoon or spider strainer, transfer the cooked rigatoni to the saucepan and proceed to "marry" the sauce and the pasta over medium-low heat, adding a bit of pasta cooking water if necessary to attain the right consistency (see Some Thoughts on Pasta, page 36).

7. Turn off the heat, add a generous handful of grated cheese (your preference: Romans would use pecorino, but Parmigiano-Reggiano is a beautiful substitute). Add a bit of olive oil and stir well to incorporate. Serve immediately in warmed bowls with additional grated cheese on top.

SALTIMBOCCA ALLA ROMANA
Veal Saltimbocca Roman-Style

I love saltimbocca. There's something irresistible about the combination of tender veal, salty prosciutto, pungent fresh sage, and a carefully emulsified white wine pan sauce that's almost transcendental. The finished whole really is greater than the sum of its parts.

Whenever we're in Rome, I am always in search of the city's best version of this classic Roman dish (and I think I may have found it recently at the legendary Roman trattoria Armando al Pantheon). Of course, like any proud Roman, Sergio claims that the best saltimbocca is the one that emerges from his home kitchen. Here's how he does it.

For the veal, ask your butcher to cut the meat from the leg, or, if you're feeling extravagant, from the tenderloin. For a slightly less rich and more economical version of the dish, substitute slices of chicken breast.

SERVES 4

8 slices young veal, pounded thin

8 fresh sage leaves

8 slices prosciutto di Parma or prosciutto di San Daniele

All-purpose flour

High-quality extra-virgin olive oil

½ cup (120 ml) white wine (anything you'd be happy to drink)

1 tablespoon (15 g) butter

1. Place the veal slices on top of one or two pieces (as needed) of plastic wrap on a flat work surface. Place a sage leaf on top of each slice and then top with a slice of prosciutto just big enough to cover.

2. Sprinkle a few drops of water on each completed veal slice (this will help later when it's time to remove the plastic wrap). Cover the veal slices with another sheet of plastic wrap. Pound each slice lightly with a meat pounder or the bottom of a pan, just firmly enough to meld together the veal, sage, and prosciutto and flatten the slice slightly.

3. Place the plastic-wrapped slices in the refrigerator for at least 1 hour. You could prepare the slices and refrigerate them for up to 8 hours before cooking. This resting time will help the prosciutto and sage adhere to the veal slices during cooking.

4. Remove the veal slices from the refrigerator and carefully peel off the top layer of plastic wrap.

5. Sprinkle the tops of the veal slices lightly with flour and gently shake each slice to evenly distribute the flour and remove any excess.

6. Heat 3 to 4 tablespoons (45 to 60 ml) of olive oil in a sauté pan over medium-high heat until the oil is shimmering. Place 3 or 4 veal slices (depending on the size of your pan—do not overcrowd the slices) into the pan, prosciutto-side down, and brown well on that side, 3 to 4 minutes. Flip the slices and cook for another 2 minutes or so, just enough to get some color on the other side of the slices. Remove the finished slices from the pan and place on a warmed plate. Repeat the process with the remaining slices of veal.

—continued—

SALTIMBOCCA ALLA ROMANA
(continued)

7. When all the veal slices have been cooked, lower the heat to medium and deglaze the pan with the white wine, allowing the wine to come up to a boil and scraping up the browned bits from the bottom of the pan with a wooden spoon. Reduce the wine by about half.

8. Add all the veal slices back to the pan, prosciutto-side up, and cook in the white wine emulsion for 1 or 2 minutes. If the sauce seems too thin, continue cooking until it's further reduced. If it seems too thick or dry, add a bit of water to the pan to reconstitute it to the desired saucy consistency. Transfer the veal slices to warmed dinner plates, 2 slices per serving. Turn off the heat under the pan, add the butter, and vigorously emulsify the butter into the pan sauce, simultaneously shaking the pan and stirring the butter into the sauce to incorporate it.

9. Spoon the finished pan sauce generously over the portioned-out veal slices. Serve immediately.

Make It a Meal: This chapter gives you all you need for a complete, authentic Roman repast. Start with a bowl of Sergio's amatriciana (page 126) and follow it with this veal classic.

Wine Pairing: Fattoria San Giusto a Rentennano "Per Carlo" IGT Toscano 2019. "Per Carlo" is a reference point for Sangiovese "in purezza" (100 percent Sangiovese) from Chianti Classico. It'll put a smile on your face with this classic Roman dish.

SABATINO AND JENNI

If you pull into Gaiole for some sightseeing, a bit of shopping, or just an evening passeggiata (loose translation: "leisurely stroll") and aperitivo, chances are good you'll find parking in the municipal lot just a stone's throw from the main piazza. Looming over the parking area is a backlit sign announcing the presence of I' Galletto 'Briaco Trattoria.

Inside is an immaculate family-run restaurant, its walls decorated with old-world farming tools and its tables covered by checkered linens. This has been the long-time domain of two husband-wife teams: Pasquale and Cecilia—the first-generation founders now enjoying retirement—and their son, Sabatino, and his wife, Jenni, who carry on the tradition. While Jenni tends to the front of the house, Sabatino runs the kitchen with steady hands, turning out thoughtfully prepared dishes. The trattoria's classics hew to Chiantigiana tradition, though Sabatino—who was formally trained at an elite hospitality school and spent time in fine-dining kitchens throughout Tuscany before returning home—pushes the envelope just a bit with innovative specials. There's something here for everyone.

GALLETTO 'BRIACO
Braised Drunken Chicken

One of the house specialties at l' Galletto is its namesake dish, the galletto 'briaco, literal translation: "drunken rooster." The recipe, a more or less well-kept secret, is a mix of herbs, aromatics, and wine that combine to produce a uniquely flavorful braise. But I believe the essence of the dish is intact in my take on the trattoria's original.

SERVES 4 TO 6

1 (4- to 6-lb/1.8- to 2.7-kg) whole chicken, backbone removed and halved

Kosher or coarse sea salt and freshly ground black pepper

2 garlic cloves, crushed

4 sprigs fresh rosemary, divided

¾ cup (180 ml) extra-virgin olive oil, divided, plus more as needed

2 cups (480 ml) dry white wine (something you'd be happy to drink)

1 lemon, cut into ½-inch (1.3-cm) slices

1. Season the chicken halves generously with salt and pepper. Place the chicken in a large plastic or nonreactive container that has a cover. Add the garlic, 2 sprigs of the rosemary, ½ cup (120 ml) of the olive oil, 1 cup (240 ml) of the white wine, and the lemon slices to the container. Mix well with your hands to thoroughly coat the chicken halves. Cover tightly and refrigerate for at least 4 hours or preferably overnight.

2. Remove the chicken from the refrigerator about 2 hours before you plan to begin cooking to bring it up to room temperature.

3. Remove the chicken from the marinade and wipe clean with paper towels.

4. In a skillet or sauté pan large enough to accommodate the two chicken halves in one layer, heat the remaining ¼ cup (60 ml) of olive oil over medium-high heat until it begins to shimmer.

5. Add the chicken halves to the pan, skin-side down, and cook until the skin takes on a deep golden-brown color, 5 to 7 minutes. Flip the chicken halves and continue cooking for another 2 minutes.

6. Add the remaining 1 cup (240 ml) of white wine to the pan, allow it to come to a boil, and scrape the bottom of the pan with a wooden spoon to loosen all the caramelized bits. When all the alcohol in the wine has burned off and you can no longer smell the vapors coming off of the pan, adjust the heat to low and cover the pan.

—continued—

GALLETTO 'BRIACO
(continued)

7. Cook at a very low simmer for about 40 minutes. Check the pan every 10 minutes or so to make sure that there is still some liquid in the bottom of the pan. You want enough liquid to continue the cooking and to eventually create a syrupy sauce for the finished dish, but not so much liquid that the final result will be watery. If necessary at any point, add 2 to 3 tablespoons (30 to 45 ml) of water to the pan to keep things from becoming too dry. Conversely, if there seems to be too much liquid in the pan, especially toward the end of the 40-minute cooking time, remove the lid from the pan and continue cooking. This should help slowly reduce the amount of liquid in the pan. Turn off the heat and let the chicken rest in the covered pan for 10 to 15 minutes.

8. Transfer the chicken halves to a warmed serving platter, spoon the pan sauce over the top, and drizzle with a bit of olive oil. Nestle the remaining 2 sprigs of fresh rosemary in beside the chicken and serve immediately family-style.

Make It a Meal: Pair this "drunken chicken" with a side of sautéed green beans, garlic, scallions, and cherry tomatoes (page 241) for a wholly satisfying dinner.

Wine Pairing: Rocca di Castagnoli Chianti Classico Riserva DOCG "Poggio A' Frati" 2018. This Chianti Classico riserva, produced just ten minutes away from Sabatino and Jenni's trattoria by one of Gaiole's signature producers, is a gutsy counterbalance to the wine and herb–marinated chicken.

SPAGHETTI NAPOLI
Spaghetti with Tomato Sauce and Burrata Cheese

Like many of the Gaiolesi friends you're meeting in this book, the I' Galletto family traces its roots back to Southern Italy. Their Campanian heritage shines through in this simple, but surprisingly delicious, dish of spaghetti topped with highest-quality burrata or buffalo mozzarella. As the heat of the pasta melts the cheese, it oozes its creamy essence into the tomato sauce. This is one of those dishes where all you really need to do is find the best ingredients possible, stay out of their way, and let them do the rest.

SERVES 4

Kosher or coarse sea salt

1 batch Basic Tomato Sauce (page 105)

1 pound (455 g) high-quality imported spaghetti (Afeltra or Mancini are favorite brands)

Freshly ground black pepper

½ cup (20 g) chopped fresh basil, plus 8 fresh basil leaves

1 cup (100 g) grated Parmigiano-Reggiano cheese

High-quality extra-virgin olive oil

4 balls (8 oz/230 g) burrata or buffalo mozzarella, at room temperature

1. Bring a large pot of salted water to a rolling boil over high heat.

2. In a large sauté pan, slowly and gently reheat the tomato sauce until it reaches a low, bubbling simmer. Taste for seasoning and, if necessary, adjust with salt and/or pepper.

3. Add the spaghetti to the boiling water and cook until almost al dente (see Some Thoughts on Pasta, page 36).

4. Add the spaghetti to the saucepan and stir well to combine and emulsify. If needed, add some of the pasta cooking water to the pan to achieve the desired consistency. Turn off the heat, add the chopped fresh basil, ½ cup (50 g) of the Parmigiano-Reggiano, and a drizzle of olive oil to the pan. Stir again to combine well.

5. Portion the finished spaghetti into four individual warmed serving bowls and immediately top each with a ball of burrata or buffalo mozzarella. I like to "crack" the ball open a bit with my fingers to release some of the cheese's milk and to jump-start its melting. Drizzle each bowl with a bit of olive oil, top with 2 basil leaves, and serve immediately.

Note: It's important that the burrata or mozzarella is at room temperature before you use it in this dish or it will not melt into the pasta as intended. Take the cheese out of your refrigerator at least 2 hours in advance.

RICCARDO DI RADDA

If you've ever visited Chianti, chances are very good that your time included a visit to the picturesque hilltop town of Radda. While some aspects of this small town belie its tourism-driven economy, its architectural and natural beauty, and a stubbornly proud local population that keeps the community grounded, combine to give this place an irresistible charm.

As you enter the outskirts and main parking area of the town—the center is hidden within and open only to pedestrians—you can't miss the prominent storefront and signs for Casa Porciatti Alimentari e Macelleria. The Porciatti family, represented today by Luciano and his sister, Anna, together with Luciano's sons Riccardo and Francesco, has been serving the Radda community for over fifty-eight years. And they do so with palpable passion, warmth, attention to detail, and creativity. Their shop is a feast for the senses, with beautifully displayed delicacies that fill the air with irresistible aromas. It's the kind of place you visit to purchase one specific item and end up leaving with dozens.

Never content to rest on their laurels, the Porciattis opened an enoteca and wine bar around the corner several years ago, thoughtfully curated and run by Riccardo. Tucked away off a small tunnel known as the Camminata Medioevale, it's a place that oozes wine country personality—vaulted ceilings, small trattoria tables, and shelves filled with bottles from every significant winemaker in Chianti as well as many from further afield. Olive oils, pastas, artisanal honeys, jarred condiments, and other culinary specialties round out Riccardo's offerings.

On a brisk fall afternoon, this is a great place for a long lunch and a bottle of wine. The menu is deep with local specialties and it's likely that whatever wine you choose, especially if it hails from one of Radda's nearby vineyards, Riccardo will personally know the winemaker and will convey to you the story behind the wine. Does it get any better?

BRASATO DI MANZO AL CHIANTI
Slow-Braised Beef Shoulder in Chianti Wine

This is one of the rotating daily specials at Riccardo's enoteca. Local beef shoulder is generously seasoned and slowly braised with aromatics in a Chianti wine sauce until fork-tender.

SERVES 4 TO 6

1 (5- to 6-lb/2.3- to 2.7-kg) beef shoulder (sometimes labeled as "chuck" in the U.S.) or deboned beef shank

Kosher or coarse sea salt and freshly ground black pepper

Extra-virgin olive oil

4 sprigs rosemary

12 shallots

1 tablespoon (15 g) high-quality tomato paste

½ bottle (375 ml) Chianti or similar red wine

1 cup (240 ml) chicken stock, beef stock, or water

½ cup (120 ml) Vin Santo (optional—for simpler method described in step 5)

Lemon juice

1. Preheat the oven to 325°F (165°C).

2. If using a whole beef shoulder, butterfly the meat carefully to open it up into a single relatively flat piece. If using deboned beef shank, simply open up the meat on a cutting board or kitchen work surface. Generously season the meat with salt and pepper. Douse the meat abundantly with olive oil. Place 2 sprigs of the rosemary on top of the meat and roll it up into a more or less uniform piece. Tie the meat securely with butcher's twine. Season the outside of the meat generously with salt and pepper. Tuck the remaining 2 sprigs of rosemary underneath the butcher's twine on the outside surface of the meat.

3. At this point, you can go one of two ways: You can use the traditional braising method with an initial browning of the meat and deglazing of the cooking vessel prior to long, low-temperature cooking; or, you can go with a simpler, but equally effective, method in which you place the meat, shallots, and olive oil in the cooking vessel and start the low-temperature cooking straight away.

4. For the traditional method: In a large casserole or cast-iron cooking vessel, heat 4 to 5 tablespoons (60 to 75 ml) of olive oil over medium heat, then brown the meat until it achieves a dark brown crust on all sides. Transfer the meat to a plate. Add the shallots and tomato paste to the pan and stir to combine. Raise the heat to medium-high and cook until the tomato concentrate becomes fragrant and the shallots soften slightly, about 2 minutes. Add the wine and deglaze the pan, stirring up any browned bits stuck on the bottom. Allow the wine to reduce to a syrupy glaze with no remaining odor of raw alcohol. Add the chicken stock, return the meat to the pot, and bring to a light boil.

5. For the simpler method: Transfer the meat to a large casserole or cast-iron cooking vessel, scatter the shallots around the meat, and pour in ½ cup (120 ml) of olive oil.

—continued—

BRASATO DI MANZO AL CHIANTI
(continued)

6. Cover the pan tightly, place on the middle rack of the oven, and bake for 3 to 4 hours, depending on the size and shape of the meat and the idiosyncrasies of your oven. Check the meat periodically to make sure that there is enough liquid remaining in the pot to keep everything moist and saucy. If necessary, add a bit of water or stock. The meat is done when it is very soft and can be easily pierced with the tines of a large fork. For the simple method, the addition of Vin Santo (the sweet dessert wine typical in the Chianti countryside) during the final hour of cooking is an optional but nice touch—I first learned of this flavor-enhancing technique from Dario Cecchini, the famous butcher in nearby Panzano.

7. Allow the meat to rest in the covered cooking vessel for at least 45 minutes.

8. Remove the meat from the pot and cut off the butcher's twine. Cut the meat into slices or pull it apart according to your preference. Place on a warmed serving platter and spoon some of the cooking liquid and braised shallots over the meat. Finish with a generous drizzle of olive oil, a sprinkling of coarse sea salt, and a light squirt of lemon juice. Serve with the remaining cooking liquid on the side.

Bonus Dish . . . Piatto di Recupero!
Leftover brasato is easily repurposed as a pasta sauce and it's especially good with rigatoni. Simply reheat and shred pieces of the meat together with some of the leftover braising liquid and a generous dose of extra-virgin olive oil in a large sauté pan. A large spoonful of Basic Tomato Sauce (page 105) is a nice—though entirely optional—addition, if there is some on hand. As needed, add some pasta cooking water to the pan to loosen and emulsify the sauce. Add the cooked pasta to the pan and marry with the sauce. Top with Parmigiano-Reggiano and serve immediately.

Another option is to shred the leftover meat and use it as a stuffed pasta filling. Combine the shredded meat with a generous amount of ricotta and Parmigiano-Reggiano cheeses, add 1 large egg, and mix well to combine into a homogeneous filling mixture. Use it to fill ravioli. The ravioli would be delicious with the Basic Tomato Sauce (page 105).

Note: This dish can be made the day before and stored in your refrigerator. Reheat in the oven for about 45 minutes before serving. It may be even better that next day.

Make It a Meal: Mashed potatoes or a risotto of your choice (page 49) would complement this hearty Chianti braise.

Wine Pairing: Rocca di Montegrossi Chianti Classico Gran Selezione DOCG "San Marcellino" 2016. The richness and depth of this beef braise call for a bold wine with equal depth and richness. This gran selezione from winemaker Marco Ricasoli Firidolfi fits the bill.

ZUPPA DI FARRO
Farro Soup

Beyond the ubiquitous (but delicious) pappa al pomodoro and ribollita soups that appear on trattoria menus throughout Chianti, you may also find grain-based soups that pack a gutsy, flavorful punch in late autumn and winter. Farro is a popular base for these soups.

Available at specialty food markets and through online sources such as Eataly and Gustiamo.com, farro has a deep nutty flavor and chewy texture that lends itself well to risotto-style soups such as the one served at Riccardo's enoteca during cold-weather months. Typically, farro can be found in small, medium, and large grain sizes, and is also distinguished by how it has been processed: whole grain, semi-whole grain (semi-pearled), or husked (pearled). The pearled version—*perlato* in Italian—is most commonly used because its cooking time is shorter.

SERVES 4

4 to 5 tablespoons (60 to 75 ml) high-quality extra-virgin olive oil, plus more as needed

1 large carrot, peeled and finely diced

1 large celery stalk, finely diced

1 yellow onion, finely diced

10 to 12 cherry tomatoes, cut in half

Kosher or coarse sea salt and freshly ground black pepper

10 ounces (280 g) farro perlato

4 to 5 cups (1 to 1.2 L) vegetable or chicken broth

½ lemon

1. In a medium stockpot, heat the olive oil over medium heat. Add the carrot, celery, onion, and cherry tomatoes. Season with some salt and a few grinds of black pepper. Stir well to coat the vegetables with the oil and distribute the salt and pepper. Cook slowly for 2 minutes.

2. Add the farro to the pot and stir well to combine with the vegetables. Raise the heat to medium-high and cook, stirring occasionally, for 2 to 3 minutes to lightly toast the farro.

3. Add enough broth to cover the farro by about 2 inches (5 cm) and lower the heat to maintain the mixture at a slow, low simmer. Cover the pot and cook for about 45 minutes, or until the farro has become soft but still retains its integrity (in other words, not mushy). Check the pot every 10 minutes or so to make sure that the farro is still barely covered in broth. If necessary, add a bit more broth. Some people enjoy this soup thick, almost the texture of a risotto. Others prefer it soupier. Add or hold back broth during the cooking time to reach your final desired result.

4. When the farro has reached the desired consistency, turn off the heat and taste for seasoning. Add salt and/or pepper if necessary, and finish with a drizzle of olive oil and a squeeze of lemon juice. Mix well. Serve in warmed bowls with another drizzle of olive oil on top.

FRANCO
(DETTO "IL BANDITO")

Situated about ten minutes outside of Gaiole, high on a ridge near the small hamlet of Castagnoli, Osteria Il Bandito is everything you could want in a simple countryside trattoria. Don't come expecting white-tablecloth dining, cutting-edge cuisine, or a wine cellar filled with Super Tuscan treasures. Do come expecting breathtaking views of the surrounding area, the distinct smell of meat being grilled over live fire, a long list of classic pasta dishes, and the ever-present grin of the osteria's chef/proprietor, Franco.

Franco—he's the "Bandito"—is an interesting guy. Sardinian by birth, he's yet another transplant to Tuscany who came to find work and has made Chianti his home for more than thirty years now. He started out in a nearby city as a bouncer at a discotheque, but eventually, maybe after the ouster of one too many unruly patrons, turned to what he really loves: food. This giant of a man loves to eat—that's obvious when you meet him—and he loves to cook to make the people around him happy.

Assisted by his son and wife, this is strictly a family affair. It's a no-frills operation that succeeds with personal attention to detail, an eye for quality ingredients, and an honest desire to present something simple but delicious every day.

Franco keeps things interesting with some dishes from the Sardinian tradition. If you call in advance, he'll proudly prepare you his famous whole roasted suckling pig in the Sardinian style. His spaghetti dello chef brings together sun-dried tomatoes, dried fruit, nuts, hot pepper, and pecorino cheese in a burst of flavor from another place. It's irresistible.

Me? I gravitate toward the Tuscan classics. This Sardinian transplant has a way with all of them.

PAPPARDELLE AL CINGHIALE
Pappardelle with Wild Boar Sauce

At some point during a Tuscan vacation, you will inevitably encounter some kind of pasta dish dressed with a wild boar sauce. It might seem off-putting, especially if you've ever met up with a wild boar or, worse yet, seen the film *Hannibal*. But I assure you, this is a dish you want to try.

Wild boar—*cinghiale* in Italian—are ubiquitous throughout the Tuscan countryside and a constant bane to local farmers and winemakers whose crops are routinely savaged by the beasts. It's a constant war of wills. The annual wild boar hunting season, typically starting in early November and continuing until the ranks are adequately thinned out, is anxiously anticipated each year. And Tuscans being Tuscans, nothing goes to waste.

Here's Franco's take on the classic.

SERVES 4 TO 6

½ bottle (375 ml) good-quality red wine (a Chianti would be ideal)

½ cup (120 ml) high-quality extra-virgin olive oil, plus more as needed

1 bay leaf (may substitute dried if unavailable)

1 sprig rosemary

10 juniper berries

1 garlic clove, finely minced

2 pounds (910 g) wild boar meat (preferably from the shoulder), cubed

2 carrots, peeled and finely diced

2 celery stalks, finely diced

2 red onions, finely diced

1 tablespoon (15 g) tomato paste

1 (28-oz/784-g) can high-quality whole San Marzano tomatoes, hand crushed with their juices

Kosher or coarse sea salt and freshly ground black pepper

1 pound (455 g) freshly made or dried pappardelle noodles (see My Way with Fresh Pasta, page 58)

1. In a large nonreactive container (a plastic storage tub with a tight-sealing cover would be ideal), mix together the red wine, ¼ cup (60 ml) of the olive oil, bay leaf, rosemary, juniper berries, and garlic. Toss in the cubed boar meat and mix everything together to thoroughly combine and coat the meat. Cover the container and place in the refrigerator overnight. Twenty-four hours of marination is ideal.

2. After the meat has been marinated, it's time to assemble and slowly cook the sauce. Heat the remaining ¼ cup (60 ml) of olive oil in a heavy-bottomed cooking vessel over medium-low heat. Add the carrots, celery, and onions and cook until the mixture becomes translucent, soft, and eventually takes on almost a copper color, 25 to 30 minutes. Be patient with this step. It's worth the effort.

3. Having achieved the right consistency with your soffritto (the Italian term for the basic carrot/celery/onion mix that forms the base of many sauces and soups), remove the boar meat from the marinade mixture, reserve the marinade, and place the meat in the pot along with the tomato paste. Mix well to coat the meat and vegetables with the tomato paste.

4. Raise the heat to medium-high and brown the meat well all over, stirring occasionally. Eventually, within 5 to 7 minutes of cooking, the tomato paste will begin to caramelize on the bottom of the pan.

—continued—

PAPPARDELLE AL CINGHIALE
(continued)

5. Add the reserved marinade mixture (be sure to remove the bay leaf first), raise the heat to high, and deglaze the pot, scraping up all the browned bits stuck to the bottom of the pot and mixing well to combine. Let the mixture bubble vigorously until the alcohol in the wine has burned off and the liquid has reduced by about half.

6. Add the tomatoes to the pot together with a few generous pinches of salt and several grinds of black pepper. Mix well to combine. Lower the heat to bring the mixture to a slow bubbling simmer. Cook, adding a bit of water occasionally if needed to keep the sauce from becoming too dry, for 3 to 4 hours, or until the boar meat becomes fork-tender.

7. Break up the boar meat with a fork or wooden spoon and mix to incorporate it into the sauce. Taste for seasoning, and if needed, add more salt and pepper. Allow the sauce to rest in the pot for at least 2 hours. This resting time will ensure a tender final consistency and a thorough melding of flavors.

8. Bring a large pot of salted water to a boil over high heat. Add the pappardelle and cook to the "punto giusto" (see Some Thoughts on Pasta, page 36).

9. While the pasta is cooking, place 3 to 4 cups (720 to 960 ml) of the finished wild boar sauce into a shallow saucepan with 3 to 4 tablespoons (45 to 60 ml) of olive oil. Heat the sauce thoroughly over medium-high heat. When it begins to bubble and stick a bit to the pan, add a generous spoonful of the pasta cooking water and continue heating and mixing.

10. Using tongs, transfer the cooked pasta to the saucepan and begin stirring vigorously to emulsify and combine the pasta with the sauce, adding, if necessary, a bit more of the pasta cooking water to achieve the desired consistency. Serve immediately in warmed bowls.

Note: It's not impossible to find wild boar in the U.S. D'Artagnan USA offers a quality product (see Sources, page 256). You could substitute ground wild boar meat for the cubed meat specified in this recipe (and many Tuscans prepare the dish that way). But I like the texture of slowly braised and broken-down shoulder meat produced by this method here. Boar meat tends to be extra tough and gamey, hence a 24-hour marinade bath is your best bet to ensure a tender and pleasantly flavorful final result.

ROSTICCIANE E SALSICCIE ALLA GRIGLIA
Grilled Pork Ribs and Sausages

Did I mention that there's a live fire grill at Il Bandito? There's something about the smell of Tuscan oak burning red hot under a cast-iron grate with meat drippings hitting the coals . . .

One of our favorite "secondi" coming off that wood-fired grill at Il Bandito is a simple plate of pork spare ribs and sausage. Ribs in the Tuscan tradition are not slow-cooked until falling off the bone as they are in the American barbecue realm (something I love back home). They are thoroughly cooked through on the grill, but retain their integrity with a pleasing snap in each bite.

SERVES 4 TO 6

2 large racks heritage pork ribs

Kosher or coarse sea salt and freshly ground black pepper

2 tablespoons (15 g) dried fennel pollen

6 pieces Italian-style sausage (hot or mild, according to your taste and mood)

Extra-virgin olive oil

1 lemon, quartered

1. Light a wood or charcoal fire in your outdoor grill. When the flames subside and the coals are red hot, the fire will be ready for cooking.

2. Season the rib racks generously on both sides with salt and pepper. Sprinkle both sides of the racks with the fennel pollen. Do not season the sausages—if they are well-prepared they will already have plenty of seasoning.

3. Grill the rib racks and sausages over the live fire, turning them from time to time so they cook evenly. It's best to go slowly. Maybe push your coals over to one side of the grill to create a "hot" zone and a "cool/indirect heat" zone. Move the meat around between the cooking zones. You want it to cook through without burning on the outside but, at the same time, you do want a nice caramelized crust on the outside. Use your common sense. Both the sausages and the ribs should be cooked through in about 30 minutes.

4. Remove the finished rib racks and sausages from the grill. Carve the ribs into single pieces, using a sharp knife to slice between each rib section. Place the ribs and sausages on a family-style serving platter. Drizzle with some olive oil and finish with a few squeezes of fresh lemon juice.

Make It a Meal: With some peperonata (page 156) and a simple salad (page 199), you've got the makings of a great meal.

Wine Pairing: Monteraponi Chianti Classico DOCG 2020. Monteraponi's wines—from nearby Radda—are gaining a cult following. Their Chianti Classico stands up to, but does not overpower, the smoky deliciousness of these grilled meats.

PEPERONATA
Braised Sweet Peppers and Onions

Almost every region of Italy seems to have some version of the classic peperonata. At its core, it's a simple sauté or braise of sweet peppers, onions, and garlic dressed with extra-virgin olive oil, basil, and a few drops of lemon juice. It pairs well with grilled meats and chicken. It's also great as a sandwich ingredient.

In Sicily, the addition of eggplant and perhaps some raisins or currants combine to create a "caponata." The variations, once you've mastered the basic recipe, are limited only by your imagination. Do you like rosemary? Substitute that for the basil, or go with both herbs. Do you prefer red onions to yellow? Red onions add a great depth of flavor—and color—to the dish. Taste as you go and make note of what works and what doesn't, what you like and what you don't. That's how to think and cook like a Tuscan.

SERVES 6

3 large red bell peppers

3 large yellow bell peppers

1 large green bell pepper

2 medium yellow or red onions

½ cup (120 ml) high-quality extra-virgin olive oil, plus more as needed

1 garlic clove, thinly sliced

2 or 3 small cherry tomatoes, halved

Kosher or coarse sea salt and freshly ground black pepper

8 to 10 basil leaves, cut into fine ribbons

½ lemon

Note: The peperonata can be made in the morning or even the day before. It stores well in the refrigerator in an airtight container for up to 1 week. Bring it to room temperature before serving.

1. Cut the tops and very bottoms off of the peppers and remove any seeds. Cut the main parts of the peppers in half and, if necessary, cut out the tough internal membranes. Cut the halved pieces into 1-by-2-inch (2.5-by-5-cm) strips. Cut additional bite-size pieces from the tops of the peppers, working around and discarding the stems. Finally, cut the bottoms of the peppers into additional bite-size pieces.

2. Peel the onions and cut them into 1-inch (2.5-cm) square pieces.

3. Heat the olive oil in a heavy-bottomed sauté pan over medium-high heat. Add the peppers, stir well to combine with the olive oil, and cook for 3 to 4 minutes to get things started.

4. Decrease the heat to medium-low, add the onions and garlic to the pan, mix well, and continue cooking for another 5 to 6 minutes.

5. Squeeze the tomatoes over the pan and add them to the pan. Add two or three generous pinches of salt and several grinds of black pepper. Stir well.

6. Add just enough water to cover the bottom of the pan. You want enough water to create a "braising situation," but not so much as to create a soupy mess. If in doubt, use less. You can always add a bit more water as you go, if necessary.

7. Decrease the heat to low, cover the pan with the top slightly ajar, and slowly braise the vegetables, stirring occasionally, until the peppers are cooked through and tender, 25 to 30 minutes longer.

8. Remove the pan from the heat, add the basil, squeeze some lemon juice into the mixture, and drizzle with a bit of olive oil. Mix well to combine all the ingredients. Taste and add more salt and pepper if needed. Allow it to cool down to room temperature before serving.

FERNANDA

Every small town in Chianti has its "go-to" family-run trattoria. Usually, you'll find it on the main piazza. It's the place you go when all you want is the familiar, when all you crave is comfort. It's where you're welcomed with a hug and a big smile. Birthdays, baptisms, first communions, and anniversaries are celebrated there. In Gaiole, it's Lo Sfizio di' Bianchi.

I'll never forget our first to visit to Lo Sfizio. It was a cold, rainy day in April and I'd planned a surprise birthday celebration for Cyndy. We'd rented a villa for the week, and six couples—all dear friends—had come to Chianti for the occasion to surprise her. But the group had run late driving from Milan-Malpensa to Tuscany. And by the time they had reached our rendezvous location, a fine-dining restaurant about 10 minutes outside of Gaiole, lunch service was over and the chef had gone home.

"Not to worry," said the restaurant's owner, "I know a place. I will call for you."

Twenty minutes later, we were all seated around a long table inside Lo Sfizio. Fernanda, one of Guido Bianchi's daughters, who now owns and runs the trattoria with her daughters, Claudia and Alessandra, and Claudia's husband, Alen, had opened up for our group and welcomed us in like family. She continues to welcome Cyndy and me like family today—some twenty years after that first happenstance lunch.

COCCOLI CON PROSCIUTTO CRUDO
Deep-Fried Dough Balls
with Prosciutto and Stracchino Cheese

When I think of classic Tuscan comfort food, one of the first that comes to mind is coccoli—literally translated as "cuddles" or "snuggles." These rustic, deep-fried balls of dough are irresistible. Typically served in trattorias and pizzerias as an antipasto or starter course, the classic way to enjoy them is with a smear of stracchino cheese—a distant relative of our American cream cheese—and a slice of prosciutto. The warm coccolo just barely melts the cheese and the salty prosciutto as you bite into it; a bit of culinary comfort on a fried dough ball.

At Lo Sfizio, pizza is served on Thursday, Friday, and Saturday nights. Any leftover dough is stored and used to make coccoli. If you're into making bread at home, you can use a portion of your dough for coccoli. If not—no worries. Some store-bought pizza dough, readily available in most supermarkets, will do the trick.

Stracchino is available online through Eataly and at artisanal cheese shops. You can substitute any smooth, spreadable cheese with a mild, tangy flavor. Or create your own substitute by combining some cream cheese with sour cream or crème fraîche to mimic the consistency and flavor profile of real stracchino.

SERVES 6 AS AN APPETIZER

4 to 6 cups (1 to 1.4 L) peanut, vegetable, or grapeseed oil (or any other neutral-flavored oil)

Just over 8 ounces (230 g) bread dough or pizza dough

Kosher or coarse sea salt

1 cup (240 g) stracchino cheese (or a close substitute)

12 slices prosciutto di Parma

1. Preheat the oven to 200°F (95°C). Line a baking sheet with paper towels.

2. Pour enough oil into a heavy-bottomed cooking vessel or cast-iron pot to reach no more than halfway up the sides. (Make sure the vessel has sufficiently high sides so there is no chance of the vigorously bubbling hot oil spilling over while frying.) Heat the oil until it reaches 360°F (185°C).

3. Break off golf ball–size pieces of the dough and either roll them neatly or, as I prefer, leave them a bit unshaped and rustic, which promotes some nice texture and pointed edges during frying.

4. Working in batches of three or four pieces at a time (if you put more in, the temperature of the oil may drop too much and you won't be able to achieve a crisp, non-oily result), and using tongs or a mesh strainer, carefully put the dough balls into the hot oil and fry, turning them often to ensure even cooking, until they reach a beautiful golden color.

5. Transfer the cooked dough balls to the paper towel–lined baking sheet. Sprinkle with salt and place them in the oven to keep them warm while you fry the rest of the dough balls.

6. When all of the dough balls have been fried, place them on a serving plate alongside the stracchino cheese and the prosciutto di Parma. Serve them while they are still warm.

SPAGHETTI AL POMODORO PICCANTE
Spaghetti with Spicy Tomato Sauce

Spaghetti. An Italian icon. Who doesn't think of spaghetti when they think of Italian food?

A simple spaghetti al pomodoro suffers from two misconceptions: It's boring and it's easy to make. Neither is true. A poorly made (or mediocre) spaghetti al pomodoro will be boring by virtue of its lack of taste, depth of flavor, and complexity. But a well-made version is a revelation.

What distinguishes a great spaghetti al pomodoro from a mediocre one? Ingredients and technique. With only a few ingredients in play—pasta, tomatoes, olive oil, a touch of garlic, maybe some chile pepper and cheese—there is no place for inferior ingredients to hide. And those ingredients need to be handled the right way, with all of the tricks of pasta "mastery" already discussed in depth throughout this book.

Lo Sfizio prepares a great spaghetti al pomodoro with a nice hit of heat (optional, of course). Here's how they do it.

SERVES 4

Kosher or coarse sea salt

½ cup (120 ml) high-quality extra-virgin olive oil, plus more as needed

1 garlic clove, thinly sliced

½ teaspoon (2 g) chopped preserved Calabrian chile pepper (optional)

1 (28-oz/784-g) can high-quality whole San Marzano tomatoes, hand crushed with their juices

Freshly ground black pepper

1 pound (455 g) high-quality spaghetti

6 fresh basil leaves, torn into small pieces

½ cup (50 g) grated Parmigiano-Reggiano cheese, plus more for serving

1. Bring a large pot of salted water to a rolling boil over high heat.

2. Heat the olive oil in a large sauté pan over low heat. Add the garlic and cook slowly, being careful not to let the garlic burn or take on too much color, which can produce bitterness in the finished sauce, until it just reaches a blondish color. Add the chile pepper (if using).

3. Add the tomatoes to the pan to stop the browning of the garlic. Add several pinches of salt and a few grinds of pepper. Stir well to combine. Raise the heat to medium-high and bring the sauce to a vigorous boil. Cook for about 5 minutes, then lower the heat to cook the sauce at a light, bubbling simmer. If the sauce seems too thick, add a bit of water to the pan to achieve the right consistency. Cook for an additional 20 minutes, or until the mixture has reached a nice "saucy" consistency. Turn off the heat, taste for seasoning, and add more salt and pepper, if needed.

4. Put the spaghetti into the boiling water and cook until al dente (see Some Thoughts on Pasta, page 36).

5. When the spaghetti has almost reached its al dente point, reheat the sauce over medium-low heat. Using tongs, transfer the spaghetti to the sauce and stir everything well to combine and emulsify. If needed, add some of the pasta cooking water to the pan to achieve the desired consistency.

6. Turn off the heat, add the basil, Parmigiano-Reggiano, and a drizzle of olive oil to the pan. Stir well again. Serve immediately in warmed bowls with extra Parmigiano-Reggiano on the side.

CARLOTTA

Friends often ask, "How can you eat Italian every night?" It's an understandable question. As Americans, we are accustomed to a melting pot–driven spectrum of culinary choices far beyond the imaginations of, not just Italians, but pretty much any nationality you can think of.

One night it's straight-up steak and potatoes; the next an Italian-American classic like chicken parm; Friday may be reserved for Chinese takeout; while Thai, sushi, Mexican, Korean barbecue, Southern fried chicken, and souvlaki are all waiting in the wings. It's one of the reasons why, in my opinion, New York City is the world's best restaurant city—the mind-blowing plethora of choices.

When here in Chianti, I fall right into the region's culinary rhythms and traditions without much longing for what I might have had for dinner on any given evening back in the U.S. But, I admit, once in a while, I do crave a great burger.

Every year, during the lead-up to Gaiole's famous "Eroica" bicycle race, dozens of pop-up food stands branch out along the town's streets. Our friend Carlotta, an energetic young woman in her thirties, and her family operate one of the most popular stands, serving up big juicy American-style griddled burgers made from 100 percent local Chianina beef.

A truly great burger is an elusive thing. It seems so simple. But it's not, as evidenced by the many disappointing burgers I've been served over the years. Great meat, a great bun, and spot-on technique are all required. Here's how it's done on Eroica weekend in Chianti.

HAMBURGER ALLA CHIANTIGIANA
Chianti-Style Griddled Burgers

At Carlotta's stand, burgers are hand-formed and then cooked on a screaming-hot griddle top. While I do enjoy the occasional burger cooked on a grill over an open flame, the griddle-top method really is the best—it preserves the burger's juices and a fair amount of fat that provides that irresistible mouthfeel. You can replicate the method at home with a well-seasoned cast-iron skillet. If you have a trusted butcher, you could request from your butcher a special blend of ground chuck and brisket.

SERVES 4 LARGE

2 pounds (910 g) 80% to 85% lean freshly ground beef

Vegetable or peanut oil

Kosher or coarse sea salt and freshly ground black pepper

Cheese of your choice (optional)

4 hamburger buns

Sliced tomato (if in season)

Sliced or diced white onion

Lettuce leaves

Assorted condiments of your choice

Beer Pairing: Birra BVS Valdarno Malafrasca. If you can't find BVS's Malafrasca to wash down this burger, don't sweat it; go with your favorite IPA instead. But do seek out artisanal Italian beers in specialty wine and beer shops. Italian producers have made big strides in quality in recent years.

1. Divide the ground beef into four equal balls, each approximately 8 ounces (230 g). Gently press each ball between your hands and work it into a 1½-inch (4-cm) thick patty. Try not to overwork the meat, just loosely pat it into place and compress it enough so it just holds its shape. Place the formed patties on a plate, cover with plastic wrap, and refrigerate for at least 1 hour. I prefer to chill for 3 hours or more. Chilling will help the burgers hold their shape during cooking and also allow for a perfect medium-rare result.

2. Heat a cast-iron skillet over high heat until it's smoking hot. Add a bit of oil to give the burgers a jump-start when they hit the hot surface.

3. Remove the burgers from the refrigerator. (Wait until the last minute to take them out of the fridge. This is probably the only time I can think of when you DO NOT want to bring your meat up to room temperature before cooking; it's just the way with burgers.) Generously season both sides of the burgers with salt and pepper.

4. Place the burgers into the skillet, leaving space between them. Resist the urge to move them during the first few minutes of cooking. Once you achieve a nice sear, the burgers will easily release from the skillet. Cook for 2 to 3 minutes, or until you've developed a nice crust on the first side. Flip the burgers and cook for 1 to 1½ minutes. The burgers should be a perfect medium-rare, but these time indications are only estimates. Your pan may be hotter or colder, your burgers may be slightly thicker or thinner. If it seems the burgers are cooking too fast or starting to burn, lower the heat a bit.

5. If using cheese, now is the time to place it on top of the burgers. To facilitate the melting of the cheese, add a few drops of water to the skillet and cover it with a lid or a large metal serving bowl.

6. Place each finished burger on top of the bottom part of a bun with the top next to it. Serve with the tomato, onion, lettuce, and condiments on the side.

CARLO

High on a hilltop above the Castello di Brolio winery sits the small hamlet of San Regolo. Not much to see here—a small church, a handful of tiny dwellings, and a smattering of rundown storage buildings. At the heart of the village is the Trattoria Carlino d'Oro, lined with neat rows of white linen–clad tables and a rear solarium-like dining room with majestic views of the vineyards and olive orchards spread out below. Open only for lunch, the trattoria caters to a mix of locals, ex-pat residents in the know, and tourists who have had the luck to stumble upon this little gem of a restaurant.

The namesake and patron of the trattoria is Carlo, or Carlino, as he was once known. It's easy to understand how he earned the nickname "Carlino d'Oro," literally "little golden Carlo." His smile, the twinkle in his eyes, and his genuine interest in every patron light up the room.

I especially remember one of our earliest visits to the trattoria. We were there with our three children. At that time, our son Jack was fourteen or fifteen years old. We had ordered a mixed Tuscan grill with side dishes, including the trattoria's irresistible french fries. Jack decided that some ketchup was in order. I asked Carlo, who speaks no English, if Jack could get some ketchup for his fries. Without missing a beat, Carlo smiled wryly and replied, "Tell your son we only serve real food here!"

Today, Carlo is well into his nineties and spends more time gardening and less time hosting. His son, Fabrizio, carries on the family tradition in the restaurant with his wife in the kitchen. Although there is a written menu, it's rarely used. Instead, Fabrizio visits each table of diners to explain the day's specials—with pride and patience. There are usually a number of seasonal specialties running the whole spectrum from antipasti to primi and on to secondi. Here are two of my favorites as prepared at the trattoria.

PENNE AL SUGO DI SALSICCIA
Penne in Sausage Ragu

The pasta dishes at Trattoria Carlino D'Oro are notable not only for their taste, but for a more idiosyncratic reason. Rather than require diners to accept the traditional pasta sauce combinations that have become unwritten doctrine—dutifully enforced by the Tuscan food police—you're read a list of the day's fresh sauces and available pasta shapes for each. You can pretty much mix and match as you please. This combination of penne and sausage ragu hews toward tradition because the Tuscan food police are usually right.

SERVES 4

Kosher or coarse sea salt

3 to 4 tablespoons (45 to 60 ml) high-quality extra-virgin olive oil, plus more as needed

4 links (about 1 lb/455 g) Italian-style sausage (hot or sweet according to your personal taste), casings removed

1 shallot, finely diced

1 batch Basic Tomato Sauce (page 105)

Freshly ground black pepper

1 pound (455 g) high-quality imported penne (Afeltra or Mancini are favorite brands)

2 cups (200 g) grated Parmigiano-Reggiano cheese, plus more as needed

1. Bring a large pot of salted water to a rolling boil over high heat.

2. Heat the olive oil in a large sauté pan over medium-high heat. Crumble the sausage into the pan and cook until it's nicely browned all over. I've found it's best to leave the sausage alone at first, until the first side develops some color, then mix and stir to brown it all over. Transfer the sausage to a plate and set aside.

3. Decrease the heat to medium-low and add the shallot to the pan. Cook, stirring occasionally, until the shallot turns translucent, about 2 minutes. Add the tomato sauce, raise the heat to medium-high, and bring to a steady boil. With a wooden spoon, scrape up any browned bits from the bottom of the pan that accumulated during the cooking of the sausage. Lower the heat to a simmer.

4. Transfer the sausage to a cutting board and roughly cut it up into smaller, uniform pieces. Add the sausage to the tomato sauce and stir well to combine. Allow the mixture to slowly simmer for about 20 minutes. If the sauce becomes too thick, add a small amount of water to the pan and continue to cook. Taste for seasoning and, if necessary, add salt and/or pepper. (Usually, given the fact that the basic tomato sauce is already seasoned, and the sausage is also well-seasoned, there should be no need for additional salt and pepper. But better to be sure.)

5. Put the penne into the boiling water and cook until almost al dente (see Some Thoughts on Pasta, page 36).

6. Use a spider strainer or slotted spoon to transfer it to the sauce and stir everything well to combine and emulsify. If needed, add some of the pasta cooking water to the pan to achieve the desired consistency. Turn off the heat, add the Parmigiano-Reggiano and a drizzle of olive oil to the pan, and stir again to combine well.

7. Portion the pasta into four warmed serving bowls and top each with an additional dusting of Parmigiano-Reggiano. Serve immediately.

BRUSCHETTE MISTE
Grilled Country Bread
with Tuscan Olive Oil and Toppings

It's hard to find a trattoria menu in Chianti whose antipasto section doesn't include some kind of bruschetta—toasted or grilled rustic country bread adorned with any one of a number of toppings and drizzled with extra-virgin olive oil. The selection at Trattoria Carlino d'Oro runs the traditional gambit from simple fett'unta (literally, an "oiled slice") to bruschetta topped with tomatoes, beans, zucchini, or a mix of house-made sausage bound together with stracchino cheese.

Find some great bread or, better yet, try your hand at making your own (page 233), and experiment with whatever you like best as a topping. This is a great way to start off any kind of meal.

SERVES 4 TO 6 AS AN APPETIZER

24 cherry tomatoes, quartered

4 to 6 fresh basil leaves, cut into thin ribbons

Kosher or coarse sea salt and freshly ground black pepper

High-quality extra-virgin olive oil

1 loaf crusty, dense country-style bread

2 garlic cloves

1. Combine the cherry tomatoes and basil in a bowl and season with salt and pepper. Drizzle them generously with olive oil and toss well to combine. Set aside to macerate for 10 to 15 minutes.

2. Cut 6 to 8 slices of country bread. Toast the slices in a toaster or grill them on both sides in a grill pan over medium-high heat. If you have access to a grill or fireplace, you can grill the bread slices over the hot coals of the fire for a smoky, charred effect.

3. Rub each grilled bread slice with a garlic clove, top with a generous helping of the tomato mixture, and drizzle with olive oil. Serve family-style on a festive platter.

Note: This same method can be applied to any number of toppings. Try roasted red peppers, sautéed Tuscan kale with a hint of tomato sauce, braised white beans with rosemary, or any other topping that appeals to you.

MATTHEW

If I had a time machine, I'd use it on occasion to transport myself back to favorite "culinary happy places" that no longer exist. Nothing lasts forever. Tastes change. Trends go in new directions. People retire, change careers, or are suddenly no longer with us.

When I'm at one of my happy places—or more importantly, with the people I love—I try to be mindful of how fragile life is and how things evolve and change right in front of our eyes. Most of the time, in the midst of the controlled chaos that is our daily lives, we don't even sense the slow changes taking place.

But enough philosophical digression. We're here to talk about food. And for me, food is very much connected to memories and, yes, to my happy places.

I first met Matthew MacCartney at his wonderful restaurant—and personal culinary happy place—Jamestown FISH, just across the bay from Newport, Rhode Island. On our first visit, it was obvious to me that something special was going on there. Though the menu took pains to state, "We are not an Italian restaurant, we are a seafood restaurant with Italian influences" (or something to that effect), the palpable Italian flair was everywhere. In the service. In the wine list. In the food.

Matthew came out to our table that first night. I guess (actually, I now know) he was wondering to himself, "Who on earth ordered that bottle of Barolo from my list tonight? No one knows that wine." That first meeting was the start of a great friendship that's been punctuated by a shared passion for all things Italian.

After seven years as owner/chef of Jamestown FISH, Matthew, whose culinary résumé includes stints at a who's who of Michelin-starred and James Beard Award–winning restaurants in New York City, France, and Italy, decided it was time for a personal change. He closed FISH and resumed full-time work as a wine professional. He's now the group director of Wine & Culinary Education for the Ocean House Collection, a group of beautiful old-world properties that have been lovingly restored in historic Watch Hill, Rhode Island.

Matthew lived in Florence for almost two years in the 1990s. He learned to speak fluent Italian. He became involved with the Slow Food movement during its infancy. And he learned the Tuscan way with food at the side of the mythical Florentine chef Fabio Picchi, owner of Cibrèo (another "happy place," but one that will never be the same with Picchi's recent passing).

At FISH, Matthew showed Rhode Islanders what sophisticated coastal Italian cooking looks like. And these two Tuscan dishes are typical of his culinary sensibilities.

CACCIUCCO
Tuscan Fish Stew

Although it went by another name at FISH, this dish was clearly Matthew's take on a classic Tuscan cacciucco—a savory fish stew. Someone from Livorno (the Tuscan port city where the dish was invented) might raise an eyebrow at Matthew's version. He's made some modifications with nods toward both France and New England. But the spirit of the dish still cries "Cacciucco!"

SERVES 4

1 (2-lb/910-g) lobster, claws, knuckles, and tail removed from the body

4 large shrimp, peeled and deveined, shells reserved

1 (15-oz/400-g) can high-quality whole San Marzano tomatoes

2 garlic cloves, crushed

¼ teaspoon (1 g) saffron

½ teaspoon (2 g) chopped preserved Calabrian chile pepper

Kosher or coarse sea salt and freshly ground black pepper

1 dozen littleneck clams, rinsed and scrubbed

1 dozen mussels, rinsed and scrubbed

1 pound (455 g) fresh cod or hake, cut into 2-by-2-inch (5-by-5-cm) pieces

Chopped fresh Italian flat-leaf parsley

High-quality extra-virgin olive oil

½ lemon

1. Split the lobster body in half and remove any roe or tomalley, which can cloud the stock and make it bitter. Place the body halves in a small stockpot together with the shrimp shells and cover by 2 to 3 inches (5 to 7.5 cm) of water. Bring to a low, bubbling boil over medium-high heat. Lower the heat to maintain a simmer and cook for about 20 minutes. During this initial simmering, add the lobster claws and knuckles at some point, cook them for about 3 minutes in the simmering broth, then remove them and set them aside. Strain the finished broth into a heavy-bottomed cast-iron cooking vessel large enough to hold all the seafood (a 5-qt/4.75-L pot is ideal).

2. Add the tomatoes, crushing them by hand as you add them, and their juice to the strained broth. Add the garlic, saffron, and Calabrian chile pepper to the broth/tomato mixture. Bring to a simmer, stir to combine, and cook for about 30 minutes. Taste for seasoning and add salt and pepper, as needed. Allow to cool for 10 to 15 minutes. Using an immersion blender, puree the contents of the pot.

3. Add the littleneck clams and mussels to the pot followed by the lobster tail (cut the tail in half for cooking), lobster claws, and knuckles. Cover the pot and cook over medium-high heat until the clams and mussels begin to open. Take a look inside the pot after 2 to 3 minutes of initial cooking to see whether the clams and mussels are opening. Add the fish pieces and shrimp to the pot, cover, and continue cooking for 4 to 6 minutes more, or until the shrimp and fish have just cooked through without any remaining sign of translucence.

—continued—

CACCIUCCO
(continued)

4. You need to be attentive here; fish cookery is very precise. Undercooked fish is a turnoff, but overcooked fish is a dry disappointment. Stop the cooking just shy of losing the last glimpse of translucence. The fish will continue to cook off the heat. Discard any clams or mussels that did not open.

5. Sprinkle the finished dish with chopped flat-leaf parsley, drizzle generously with extra-virgin olive oil, and finish with a squeeze or two of fresh lemon. Serve directly from the pot at your table into warmed bowls alongside a generous platter of grilled or toasted bread (page 182).

Make It a Meal: Pair this Tuscan coastal classic with grilled fett'unta (page 182) to serve as a delicious mop for the savory broth.

Wine Pairing: Castello di Ama Rosato "Purple Rose" IGT Toscano 2023. Rather than a white, this delicious rosé has the added structure and body to make it the perfect partner for this hearty fish stew.

BRANZINO AL FORNO
Whole Roasted Mediterranean Sea Bass

It's hot in Chianti in the summertime. Really hot. Though the evenings are pleasant, with soft breezes and skies so full of stars you're awestruck, the oppressiveness of the midday heat drives you inside—or to the beach.

Castiglione della Pescaia lies about an hour southwest of Gaiole in the province of Grosseto. It's a favorite seaside getaway for Chiantigiani looking for a break from the inland heat and craving fresh seafood. The local markets and restaurants offer a dazzling array of both shellfish—clams, mussels, shrimp, langoustines—and seafood species local to the Mediterranean waters. Perhaps none is more common, well known, and delicious than the local sea bass, or branzino.

One lazy summer afternoon at their home in Jamestown, Rhode Island, Matthew and his wife, Pam, prepared us an amazing lunch, including a whole roasted branzino in a style typical of small trattorias on the Tuscan coast. It's easy to do and the result is delicious. Yes, it'll take some practice to master filleting the fish, but there's something about cooking a whole fish on the bone that produces a juicy, mouthwatering result difficult to otherwise duplicate.

SERVES 4

2 whole branzino (Mediterranean sea bass)

Kosher or coarse sea salt and freshly ground black pepper

High-quality extra-virgin olive oil

3 garlic cloves, 1 thinly sliced, 2 whole and unpeeled

1 lemon, thinly sliced, plus ½ lemon

3 sprigs rosemary

3 sprigs thyme

3 medium Yukon gold potatoes, very thinly sliced

16 to 20 cherry tomatoes

1. Preheat the oven to 375°F (190°C).

2. Rinse off the branzino inside and out to eliminate any clinging scales and flush out any residual blood that might be present in the body cavity. Pat dry with paper towels.

3. Season the body cavities with salt and pepper and drizzle with some olive oil. Stuff the cavities with the sliced garlic, sliced lemon, and 1 sprig each of rosemary and thyme. Generously drizzle the outside of the branzino on both sides with olive oil and season with salt and pepper.

4. In a roasting pan large enough to accommodate both branzino, toss in the sliced potatoes, cherry tomatoes, whole garlic cloves, remaining 1 sprig of rosemary, and remaining 1 sprig of thyme. Season well with salt and pepper and drizzle generously with olive oil. Toss everything together well to distribute the oil, salt, and pepper evenly. Spread out the mixture evenly on the bottom of the roasting pan.

—continued—

BRANZINO AL FORNO
(continued)

5. Place the two branzino on top of the potato/tomato mixture in the roasting pan. Roast on the middle rack of the oven until the fish is just cooked through, 20 to 25 minutes. You can check for doneness by inserting a sharp knife into the thickest part of the flesh, and then carefully touching the blade against your lip. If it's reasonably warm to the touch, the fish should be cooked through. If it's still tepid or cold, the fish need more time in the oven. You can also just "cheat" a bit by cutting into the fish and looking to see if it's lost its translucence. Stay diligent—you want to get the branzino just to the point of being cooked through. Too much cooking and it will be dry.

6. Place one of the finished branzino on a cutting board. Cut into one side of the fish just below the gills and head until you touch the central bone. Do the same near the tail. With a spoon or knife, remove the upper fins along with a fair portion of the nearby flesh, which can tend to contain bones. Do the same in the belly area of the fish. Carefully peel back the skin from the top fillet that has been created by the prior cutting and trimming. Lift the fillet off of the bone and place it on a warmed serving platter. Pull the entire bone structure away from the fish to expose the lower fillet of the fish. Carefully separate the lower fillet from the bottom side of skin and transfer it to the serving platter. Repeat the process for the other fish.

7. Scatter the potatoes, cherry tomatoes, and herbs around and over the fish fillets. Scoop up the accumulated pan juices and spoon them over the branzino fillets. Finish with a generous drizzle of olive oil and a squeeze of lemon juice.

Wine Pairing: Brovia Roero Arneis DOCG 2022. Italy's Piedmont region—tucked up in the northwest corner of the boot—is known for its world-class reds: Barbera, Barbaresco, and Barolo. But this beautiful Arneis shows that Piemontese producers are also turning out elegant white wines.

FETT'UNTA
Grilled Country Bread with Garlic and Olive Oil

Fett'unta—literally, "oiled slice"—what could be simpler? A slice of great country bread, grilled over live embers or toasted until just a bit charry, rubbed with some garlic, generously drenched with high-quality extra-virgin olive oil, and finished with a bit of sea salt. This is the perfect accompaniment to any dish that leaves you with a sauce begging to be sopped up and further enjoyed even after the main event is over.

    Your fett'unta will only be as good as the bread you use, so look for a great artisanal loaf (or bake your own on page 233) readily available in better-quality supermarket bakery sections or from any one of the many artisanal bakeries sprouting up around the U.S.

SERVES 6

6 (1-inch/2.5-cm) thick hand-cut slices of artisanal-quality country or Italian-style bread

1 garlic clove

High-quality extra-virgin olive oil

Kosher or coarse sea salt

1. Grill the bread slices on both sides over a live fire or on a gas grill. You want a medium-high heat to achieve some nice, dark grill marks without burning the bread. If your fire is too hot, the bread will burn rather than toast. If you don't have access to a grill, a grill pan is a great alternative or simply toast the bread in your toaster.

2. Rub each grilled slice on one side with the garlic clove. It's sort of a sandpaper-effect seasoning method. Don't overpower the slices with garlic; just a hint of garlic on each slice is enough.

3. Generously douse each slice of toasted bread with olive oil, sprinkle with salt, and serve.

FRANCO

The Castello di Brolio winery, in the heart of the Comune di Gaiole, is the birthplace of Chianti. The Ricasoli family has been making wine there for more than four hundred years. Their ancestor and family patriarch—Barone Bettino Ricasoli—is widely credited with developing the blend of Sangiovese and other indigenous Tuscan grape varieties that became first the preferred formula and later the legal standard by which Chianti wines were once made.

A visit to the Brolio property offers a chance to soak in the history of the Chianti Classico wine region with a tour of the family's ancient castello and to sample the Ricasoli family's impressive portfolio of wines in their tasting room. And if you're in the know, it's also a chance to sample some great local food at the property's Osteria di Brolio.

The osteria's heart, soul, and executive chef is a young Tuscan named Franco Sangiacomo. Born and raised in Colle di Val d'Elsa, Franco has spent time in prestigious kitchens both in Italy and the U.S., including the storied two-Michelin star Ristorante Arnolfo in his hometown. At Osteria di Brolio, Franco presents a refined, yet rustic, take on Tuscan classics in a comfortable, casual, and welcoming space.

Any visit to central Tuscany would feel incomplete without at least one meal centered around the region's famous bistecca alla fiorentina. I think Franco's version is one of Chianti's best, offering both sirloin and tenderloin sections on the bone. The artisanally raised beef is sourced from local farmers and prepared simply, but carefully, in accordance with time-honored traditions.

BISTECCA ALLA FIORENTINA
Grilled Porterhouse Steak in the Florentine-Style

"La fiorentina" is by definition what we know as a porterhouse steak, but a great bone-in rib-eye is a fine substitute if you can't find a porterhouse or if your taste runs toward this well-marbled cut.

In Tuscany, the thought of serving a 16-ounce (455-g) steak to a single diner (as we do at steakhouses throughout the U.S.) would never occur to a right-minded chef. A typical fiorentina will weigh in at about 2.2 pounds (1 kg) and will be sliced tableside to serve four or five people.

The key to this iconic dish really is finding the right steak. True, some basic cooking technique and skill are required. But with the right raw material, all you really need to do is not mess things up. Find an artisanal butcher shop (or order online from one of the many great meat sources that ship all over the U.S.) and spend the extra dollars for prime dry-aged beef that's been raised on a healthy diet. It will make all the difference in your fiorentina results.

SERVES 4 OR 5

2 (16- to 18-ounce/455- to 500-g)
    prime dry-aged porterhouse steaks

Kosher or coarse sea salt

Freshly ground black pepper

2 sprigs rosemary

High-quality extra-virgin olive oil

½ lemon

1. Remove the steaks from your refrigerator at least 1 hour, and preferably 2 hours, before you plan to grill them so that they warm up to room temperature.

2. Light a wood or charcoal fire in your outdoor grill (alternatively, you can use a gas grill preheated to high; or, if an outdoor grill is unavailable, preheat a ridged grill pan over high heat on your stovetop).

3. Season the meat generously with salt on both sides.

4. Grill the steaks over high heat to sear them and develop an initial crust on each side. Move the steaks to a cooler part of the grill (or lower the heat under your grill pan) and continue cooking, turning the steaks occasionally to ensure the meat cooks evenly. Your target is a medium-rare internal temperature, 8 to 9 minutes of total cooking time, depending on the heat of your fire and the thickness of your steaks.

—continued—

BISTECCA ALLA FIORENTINA
(continued)

5. You could insert a meat thermometer into the steaks to check where things are at; for medium-rare, I would pull the steaks from the grill at an internal temperature of 128°F (53°C). If you don't have a meat thermometer, you can use what I call the "touch test." Simply press the steak with your forefinger. If it's still quite "mushy," it's not done yet. You're looking for some resistance, but not too much, when you touch the steak. "Flabby" or "mushy" equals underdone (unless you prefer your steak blood-red rare as the Tuscans actually do). Rock solid to the touch equals overdone. You're after that beautiful middle ground where there's just some resistance. Keep in mind, if grilling a porterhouse, that the fillet side of the steak will cook faster than the sirloin, so try to keep the fillet over a lower heat section of your cooking surface.

6. Remove the steaks from the grill when they have reached the right internal temperature and allow them to rest on a cutting board for 5 minutes.

7. Carve the meat off the bones and cut it into slices against the grain. Place the slices on a warmed serving platter, sprinkle with a bit more salt and three or four grinds of black pepper. Nestle the rosemary sprigs in among the steak slices so that their oils and fragrance will find their way into the flavor of the meat. Drizzle with olive oil and a few squeezes of fresh lemon juice. Serve immediately.

Make It a Meal: Roasted potatoes (page 201) or slow-cooked white beans (page 191) are the traditional contorni for a fiorentina. Add some sautéed spinach (page 240) for good measure.

Wine Pairing: Castello di Brolio Chianti Classico Gran Selezione DOCG "Colledilà" 2016. This gran selezione (100 percent Sangiovese) wine leans toward the modern end of the winemaking spectrum and is made from grapes grown just down the hill from Franco's restaurant on the Brolio estate. There's a touch of new oak with undertones of vanilla that lends itself to this hearty steak dish.

FAGIOLI IN UMIDO
Slow-Cooked Tuscan White Beans

These slow-cooked beans are the traditional accompaniment to bistecca alla fiorentina, but they are also great as a side dish with braises and roasts.

It's best to start these beans at least two days before you plan to serve them. This will give you time to soak them overnight, cook them the next day, and let them sit in the refrigerator for an additional twelve to twenty-four hours. The extra resting time will allow for complete hydration of the beans and absorption of the flavors of the aromatics and seasoning. The beans should be soft and creamy but should also retain their shape.

Cooked beans can be stored in your refrigerator in a sealed plastic container for up to a week. Simply reheat when ready to serve.

**SERVES 6 TO 8
AS A SIDE DISH**

2 cups (180 g) dry cannellini or navy beans

2 tablespoons (30 ml) extra-virgin olive oil, plus more as needed

1 garlic clove, thinly sliced

2 springs fresh rosemary

2 springs fresh sage

Kosher or coarse sea salt and freshly ground black pepper

1. Rinse the beans thoroughly under cold water to remove any dirt or debris. Place the beans in a large bowl and cover them with enough water to submerge them completely. Soak the beans overnight. This softens the beans and partially rehydrates them.

2. After soaking, drain the beans and rinse them again thoroughly under cold water.

3. In a Dutch oven or large pot, heat the olive oil over medium-low heat. Add the garlic to the pot and sauté until the garlic just begins to take on a golden color, 2 to 3 minutes.

4. Add the beans, rosemary, and sage to the pot. Stir well to combine and coat everything in the olive oil.

5. Add enough water to the pot to fully submerge the beans by about 2 inches (5 cm). Raise the heat to medium-high and bring the water to a boil. Decrease the heat to low so that the beans cook at a bare, bubbling simmer. Skim off and discard any foam that rises to the surface during cooking. Usually, this occurs during the first 30 minutes or so of cooking.

—continued—

FAGIOLI IN UMIDO
(continued)

6. Continue cooking the beans, stirring occasionally, until they are soft and tender. This can take anywhere from 1 to 1½ hours or even longer. Add more water if at any time it is needed to keep the beans fully submerged.

7. Once the beans are tender, allow them to cool for about 30 minutes. Scoop out about ¾ cup (180 ml) of the beans and place them in a bowl or tall container. Puree to a smooth consistency with an immersion blender. If you don't have an immersion blender, you can use a regular blender or a food processor. Or you can just break the beans up and mash them using a fork or other utensil. Add the bean puree back to the pot with the rest of the beans. Stir well.

8. Season the beans with salt and pepper to taste. Given the volume of beans, you may have to add more seasoning than you might initially think. Accordingly, start with a restrained hand, taste as you gradually season, and adjust as necessary.

9. At this point, it's best to store the beans in the refrigerator for an additional 24 hours to fully hydrate and absorb the seasoning. You could simply place a cover on the cooking vessel and put it in the fridge or transfer the beans to a sealable plastic container.

10. When ready to serve, simply reheat the beans and serve warm with a drizzle of extra-virgin olive oil on top of each serving.

CYNDY

Where do I even start? My life partner for the past forty-plus years, my soulmate, my best friend, my wife. Always smiling. Always curious. Always ready to help anyone in need. Overflowing with love—for our children, for our extended family, for our friends. And my coconspirator in all things culinary, whether dining out or cooking in. Unless a DNA test eventually proves otherwise, I'm pretty confident that there is not a drop of Italian blood running through Cyndy's veins. But that hasn't stopped her from wholeheartedly embracing our life in Italy and all things Italian. Nor has it stopped her from becoming a great Italian cook.

Here is a selection of Cyndy's favorite dishes.

PICI CASARECCI
Handmade Pici Pasta with Rustic Spicy Tomato Sauce

Throughout the province of Siena, you'll find a pasta called *pici*. These long, curly, handmade strands have an unmistakable toothsome texture that lend themselves to a variety of sauces. In local restaurants you'll see pici cacio pepe (a simple preparation made with nothing more than pecorino cheese, freshly ground pepper, and pasta cooking water), pici al ragu, and pici all'aglione (literally "the big garlic one").

Cyndy often prepares a killer version of pici casarecci—a simple version made with a spicy tomato sauce. In her iteration of the dish, Cyndy uses fresh cherry tomatoes for some extra texture that works especially well with the pici. Usually, she makes the sauce ahead of time, whenever a bunch of harvested cherry tomatoes may be in danger of overripening, and then turns it into a delicious spur-of-the moment dinner. While not easy to find in the U.S., pici has started turning up in specialty markets and from sources such as Eataly.

SERVES 4

Kosher or coarse sea salt

½ cup (120 ml) high-quality extra-virgin olive oil, plus more as needed

1 garlic clove, thinly sliced

½ teaspoon (2 g) chopped preserved Calabrian chile pepper

24 cherry tomatoes, halved

Freshly ground black pepper

1 teaspoon (5 g) tomato paste

5 or 6 fresh basil leaves

1 pound (455 g) pici

½ cup (250 g) grated Parmigiano-Reggiano cheese, plus more for serving

1. Bring a large pot of salted water to a rolling boil over high heat.

2. In a large sauté pan, heat the olive oil together with the sliced garlic over low heat. Be careful not to let the garlic burn or take on too much color, which can produce a bitterness in the finished sauce. You want the garlic slices to cook slowly until they reach a blondish color. Add the Calabrian chile pepper and stir to combine.

3. Add the cherry tomatoes to the pan and continue to cook. Add several pinches of salt, a few grinds of pepper, and the tomato paste. Stir well to combine. Maintain the low heat and slowly cook the tomatoes until they become soft and begin to melt into a saucy consistency, 20 to 25 minutes. If the sauce seems too thick, add a bit of water. Turn off the heat, taste, and add more salt and pepper, if needed. Add the basil leaves to the sauce and stir to combine.

4. Put the pici into the boiling salted water and cook until they reach the "punto giusto" (see Some Thoughts on Pasta, page 36). This is one pasta that even in its dried form should not be served al dente.

5. When the pici is almost done, bring the sauce back up to heat. Using tongs, remove the pici from the boiling water and add them to the saucepan. Stir everything well to combine and emulsify. If needed, add some of the pasta cooking water to the pan to achieve the desired consistency. Pici will typically absorb quite a bit of liquid before reaching that perfect stage of emulsification. Turn off the heat and add the Parmigiano-Reggiano and a drizzle of olive oil to the pan. Stir again to combine well. Serve immediately in warmed bowls with extra Parmigiano-Reggiano on the side.

L'INSALATA DI CYNDY
Cyndy's Special Salad

We are fortunate to have a working vegetable garden on our property in Gaiole. It's not huge, but it's efficient and it's productive. The first things to sprout every spring/early summer are the lettuces—romaine, bibb, frisée. They're at their best at the "baby stage," big enough to justify picking them, but still small enough that they're tender and sweet.

Our friend Riccardo's wine shop stocks many artisanal food products, including olive oils and vinegars. It was there that Cyndy first discovered aceto balsamico bianco—white balsamic vinegar. It's light in color and light in body as well—not at all syrupy like its more well-known cousin. And it has a slightly sweet—yet acidic—flavor profile that's hard to describe but immediately addictive. It's become the key ingredient in a salad dressing that Cyndy has developed to showcase our early-season lettuces. Our Italian friends always ask, "Ma che c'è in questo condimento?" (What's in this salad dressing?) "È buonissimo!"

SERVES 4 AS AN APPETIZER OR SIDE DISH

1 small head romaine lettuce

1 small head bibb lettuce

1 small head frisée lettuce

1 small red onion, halved and thinly sliced

Kosher or coarse sea salt and freshly ground black pepper

½ cup (120 ml) white balsamic vinegar (Leonardi brand from Modena if you can find it)

¼ cup (60 ml) high-quality extra-virgin olive oil

Parmigiano-Reggiano cheese (optional)

Make It a Meal: This salad is great as a starter on its own or as a contorno with roast chicken (page 211), grilled meat (pages 67 and 187), or a braise (page 143).

1. Carefully pull the lettuce leaves from their cores, thoroughly wash them to remove any dirt or grit, dry them with a salad spinner or paper towels, and tear into bite-size pieces. Place in a large bowl with the sliced onion. The bowl should be large enough to comfortably allow for the mixing of the lettuces with the salad dressing.

2. In a small bowl, combine a pinch of salt, several grinds of fresh pepper, and the white balsamic vinegar. Whisk well to combine.

3. Slowly and steadily drizzle the olive oil into the bowl with one hand while simultaneously whisking vigorously with the other hand (it helps to place the bowl on top of a kitchen towel to keep it in place as you whisk). You want to emulsify the dressing into a homogenous mix of all the ingredients. Taste the dressing. If it seems to need more acid, add a bit more vinegar. If it seems too acidic, add a bit more oil. Add more salt or pepper, if needed. Whisk again to re-emulsify.

4. Pour about half the dressing on top of the lettuces and mix well to combine and fully coat the lettuces. Add more of the dressing, if needed. The lettuces should be fully coated but not swimming in dressing. Top with a bit of grated Parmigiano-Reggiano cheese, if using, and serve immediately. The salad is best prepared right at the time of serving.

PATATE ARROSTO
Oven-Roasted Potatoes

The menu in a Tuscan trattoria is classically divided into five sections: antipasti, primi, secondi, contorni, and dolci. The antipasti are what we'd call starters or appetizers. The primi include soups, risottos, and pasta dishes. Secondi span meat dishes, poultry, game, and fish. Dolci are the desserts. And the contorni are side dishes or accompaniments to the secondi.

Among the most common contorni in trattorias throughout Tuscany are roasted potatoes, patate arrosto. Typically served with meat, the potatoes—when roasted properly—are crispy on the outside, tender on the inside, and well seasoned with salt and optional garlic and rosemary. This side dish screams Tuscany!

Cyndy has perfected these potatoes, which seem easy to make but are deceptively tricky to get right. In her view, the key is olive oil—lots of it.

**SERVES UP TO 6
AS A SIDE DISH**

6 large Yukon gold potatoes
(about 3 lb/1.4 kg)

High-quality extra-virgin olive oil

Kosher or coarse sea salt and freshly
ground black pepper

3 or 4 garlic cloves, unpeeled and
smashed (optional)

3 or 4 sprigs rosemary (optional)

1. Place the potatoes in a large pot and cover them completely with water. Bring to a boil over high heat. Lower the heat to maintain a slow, steady boil and cook the potatoes until you can pierce one completely through with a skewer with little to no resistance, 30 to 45 minutes. Transfer the potatoes to a bowl or plate to cool. (This step can be done up to several hours in advance.)

2. Preheat the oven to 450°F (230°C).

3. When the potatoes have cooled enough to be handled, peel off the skins and cut the potatoes into medium-size chunks. Typically, depending on their size, you'll yield four to six chunks per potato. Place the chunks in a colander and shake them around to rough them up a bit; this helps create an ideal surface on which to get a crispy exterior.

4. Place the potatoes on a large, shallow sheet pan (a high-sided roasting pan will not work as well; the potatoes will tend to steam rather than crisp up). Douse the potatoes generously with olive oil and season well with salt and pepper. Add the garlic cloves and rosemary sprigs, if using. Mix everything well with your hands to ensure the potatoes are very well coated with olive oil. Place the sheet pan in the bottom third of the oven (this will help promote the proper crisping of the potatoes).

—continued—

PATATE ARROSTO
(continued)

5. Check the potatoes after the first 10 minutes of roasting. They should just be starting to crisp up at the bottom. If the crisping has progressed well, turn the potatoes and mix well using a spatula. If they're not yet crisping, give them another 5 minutes and check on them again.

6. Continue to check the potatoes every 5 minutes. This diligence will pay off. As the potatoes continue to become crispy on one or two sides, continue to turn them frequently with the spatula, mixing and turning to keep everything well coated with oil. The potatoes will absorb some of the oil during the roasting. If the baking sheet seems to be drying out, add another generous dousing of oil and mix well.

7. When the potatoes have crisped up nicely on two or three sides, they're done. The approximate roasting time to achieve this result should be 30 to 40 minutes.

8. Transfer the finished potatoes to a warmed serving platter, mix one more time to redistribute the olive oil evenly on the potatoes, and serve immediately.

BUDINO AI LAMPONI
Raspberry Bread Pudding

Tuscans are not big dessert people. Yes, the occasional afternoon gelato is popular. And the ubiquitous tramisù is a staple on local trattoria menus. But honestly, fresh fruit is generally the preferred end to a nice meal.

That said, our Tuscan friends do answer their sweet tooth cravings when they see something special. And Cyndy's budino ai lamponi (a bread pudding, as we know it) is a special treat.

SERVES 6 TO 8

FOR THE RASPBERRY SAUCE

4 pints (960 g) raspberries

1 cup (200 g) sugar

2 tablespoons (30 ml) water

FOR THE PUDDING

1 large baguette or similar-style loaf white bread

4 whole eggs

2 egg yolks

1¾ cups (350 g) sugar

2 cups (480 ml) whole milk

2½ cups (600 ml) heavy cream

2 teaspoons (10 ml) vanilla extract

To make the raspberry sauce:

1. Place 3 pints (720 g) of the raspberries, the sugar, and the water in a saucepan and stir to combine. Bring to a boil over medium-high heat. Lower the heat to maintain a simmer and continue cooking and stirring until the sugar has melted and you've achieved a syrupy consistency, about 10 minutes. Turn off the heat, add the remaining 1 pint (240 g) of raspberries to the mixture, and stir gently to combine. Set aside and allow the mixture to cool.

To make the pudding:

2. Preheat the oven to 325°F (165°C).

3. Cut the bread into 2-inch (5-cm) cubes and place them in an 8-by-10-inch (20-by-25-cm) ceramic baking dish.

4. Place the whole eggs, egg yolks, and sugar in a bowl and whisk until well combined and pale in color. Add the milk, heavy cream, and vanilla and whisk well to incorporate all of the ingredients. Let sit for 10 minutes or so.

5. Pour the mixture over the bread cubes. Push the bread cubes down as necessary to get them well soaked. Let soak for at least 10 minutes or up to 1 hour.

6. Dot the top of the bread pudding mixture with dollops of the raspberry syrup. Push the dollops down a bit into the mixture, but do not stir.

—continued—

BUDINO AI LAMPONI
(continued)

7. Place the baking dish in a roasting pan and fill the roasting pan with water until it reaches about one-third of the way up the sides of the baking dish. Bake for 30 minutes. Turn the roasting pan around in the oven and bake for an additional 30 minutes. Check the bread pudding for consistency. It should be firmed up with a slight jiggle when touched. If it needs more time, continue to bake for another 5 to 10 minutes, but take care not to overcook the pudding, which will cause it to have a "curdled" texture.

8. Remove the baking dish from the water bath and set it aside to cool. Serve warm in individual bowls. Alternatively, you could refrigerate the cooled pudding, remove it from the fridge about 1 hour prior to serving, and serve at, or close to, room temperature.

MY TWO CENTS' WORTH . . .

I love nothing more than diving into a cooking project in our Tuscan kitchen. Living here, I've learned so much—a lot of it from the friends you've met in this book—about drawing flavor out of simple ingredients. It's a pleasure and an honor to be able to cook here. The availability of fresh, artisanal products is an inspiration. I seem to discover something new all the time.

I have my favorites and my go-to dishes. I sometimes add my own twist, just as I hope you will as you get more comfortable in the kitchen and riff on the recipes I've shared. Here are a few of my takes on some classic Tuscan dishes as well as some other off-the-beaten-path favorites.

POLLO
Chicken

On our first trip to Florence, many years ago, we passed by a small storefront in the Santa Maria Novella neighborhood not far from the central train station. Behind a large window on one side of the shop was a brick-lined grill. Smoldering oak embers provided a low, constant heat for a rotisserie setup above. A dozen small chickens were secured to a series of long skewers, slowly turning, taking on a beautiful golden color and dripping fat into a pan below in which potatoes had been placed. The aroma—even from outside—was irresistible.

We stepped inside, where we found a large glass case filled with chickens and other meats that had been prepared on the rotisserie together with many contorni—sautéed greens, potatoes, roasted peppers, and deep-fried fritters.

We bought a chicken, and with nowhere to sit inside, took our impromptu lunch to the nearby piazza, where we perched ourselves to dig in (something, I would later find out, any self-respecting Florentine would never do; outdoor eating is strictly limited by the Tuscan "food police" to picnics and an occasional panino or gelato on the go). The intense flavor of that chicken, a combination of the quality of the bird itself, impeccable cooking technique, and a hint of smoke from that Tuscan oak-fueled fire is one of those food memories that stays with you forever and changes the way you look at a particular dish.

Since that happenstance rotisserie chicken encounter, I've been on the hunt for the perfect at-home chicken preparation. I've tried them all: my own rotisserie chicken, simply grilled, oven roasted, sautéed, and stewed. They all have their time and place, depending on your mood and the effort you want to put in. Here are a few of my favorites.

POLLO ARROSTO AL MODO MIO
Roast Chicken My Way

I roast a chicken at least once a week. It's easy to do, it fills your kitchen with delicious anticipatory aromas, and the final result is a homey, deeply comforting meal to be shared with family and friends.

When it comes to roast chicken, keep it simple. I've tried all kinds of roasting techniques and tricks, all intended to solve the eternal chicken-roasting dilemma: how to cook the dark meat thighs and legs thoroughly without overcooking the white meat breast. I've tried turning the bird periodically during roasting, tenting the breast with aluminum foil, experimenting with oven temperature (high and low), and even changing oven temperature during roasting. None of them were, in my opinion, worth the effort and bother.

For the best result, it's well worth the effort to dry brine your chicken for at least a few hours, ideally overnight. Many recipes call for wet brining in a solution of salt, sugar, and aromatics dissolved in water. Personally, I don't think it's worth the effort. A simple dry brining does the trick.

Here's my straightforward method for great roast chicken.

SERVES 4

1 (4- to 6-lb/1.8- to 2.7-kg) whole
    chicken

Kosher or coarse sea salt

½ lemon

1 sprig rosemary

1 sprig sage

1 garlic clove, unpeeled

To dry brine the chicken:

1. Season the chicken aggressively inside and out with salt. You almost can't oversalt a chicken. Be very generous and assertive with the salting; it makes all the difference in taste.

2. Stuff the seasoned chicken with the lemon half, rosemary, sage, and garlic clove. Truss the bird with butcher's twine to create a compact shape for even roasting. The most important thing is to secure the legs together and close the chicken cavity, plumping the breast as best you can.

3. Place the seasoned and trussed bird on a wire rack placed in a sheet pan. Put the pan in the refrigerator, uncovered, for at least 2 hours, and preferably up to 24 hours. Remove from the refrigerator at least 1 hour before roasting.

To roast the chicken:

4. Preheat the oven to 475°F (245°C).

5. For best roasting results, place the chicken in a cast-iron skillet—it's the best for evenly conducting heat through the bird during roasting. If you don't have a cast-iron skillet, use a roasting pan. No need for any oil or butter on the chicken, as the bird will self-baste during roasting and develop a beautiful crisp skin.

—continued—

6. Roast until the chicken is cooked through, 50 to 60 minutes, depending on the size of the chicken. Check in on the chicken after about 30 minutes of roasting. Turn the skillet or roasting pan around in the oven to even out exposure to oven "hot spots." The chicken is done when you tilt the pan and clear juices run out of the cavity of the bird. If the juices run pink, you need a bit more time to ensure the thighs and legs are cooked through.

7. When the chicken is done, remove it from the oven, place it on a cutting board, and allow it to rest for at least 15 minutes or up to 30 minutes.

8. Carve the chicken. Cut the thighs/legs away from the body, then separate the thighs from the drumsticks. Cut the breasts/wings away from the breastbone, working carefully along both sides of the breastbone with your knife. Cut the wings away from each breast half and cut each of the breast halves in two. Serve family-style on a warmed platter.

To make an optional pan sauce:

9. If you've judged things correctly, your roast chicken should be plenty juicy just the way it is. But, if you're in the mood to gild the lily a bit, a great pan sauce is just minutes away. While your chicken rests, place the cast-iron skillet or roasting pan on your stove over medium-high heat. When things get sizzling, deglaze with white wine, chicken stock, or, if neither is at hand, just plain old water. Reduce the liquid by half, strain, and taste for seasoning. Another option is to add a pat of butter after reducing the liquid and swirl it around to combine. Or add a teaspoon of Dijon mustard and stir to combine. Serve in a warmed bowl next to the roast chicken.

Make It a Meal: This simple roast chicken can be enjoyed with any of the contorni described on pages 240 through 245 to make a perfect Sunday dinner.

Wine Pairing: I Sodi Chianti Classico Riserva DOCG 2020. The small I Sodi estate is an under-the-radar Gaiole gem. Their riserva pairs well with any roast meat, including this chicken.

Bonus Dishes . . . Piatti di Recupero!

Make Stock. A roast chicken dinner—at a minimum—also produces a delicious homemade stock. It's so simple to do. Place the chicken carcass and any leftover bones in a Dutch oven or stockpot and cover with water. Place it, uncovered, in a 200°F (95°C) oven overnight. The next morning, add some chopped carrots, celery, onion, and leeks—or whatever aromatic vegetables you happen to have on hand—to the pot and bake in the oven for an additional 1½ hours. Remove the chicken carcass and bones from the pot, then scoop out as many of the vegetables as you can with a mesh strainer. Strain the finished stock into storage containers. The stock can be stored in the refrigerator for up to 1 week or frozen for as long as 3 months without sacrificing any taste.

Make Meatballs. If you have leftover chicken meat, it can easily be transformed into some delicious chicken meatballs. Pull the chicken meat off of any remaining bones and mince it finely with a sharp kitchen knife. Place the minced meat in a large bowl together with 1 egg, ½ cup (50 g) Parmigiano-Reggiano cheese, 2 cups (50 g) white bread (crusts removed) that has been soaked in milk, ¼ cup (10 g) chopped fresh Italian flat-leaf parsley, and a few grinds of black pepper. Mix thoroughly by hand until you have a well-homogenized mass. With wet hands, form small meatballs. Refrigerate the meatballs for at least 1 hour. Cook in a 425°F (220°C) oven for about 15 minutes until nicely browned. Alternatively, slowly braise the meatballs in a simple tomato sauce for no more than 20 minutes.

POLLO SPACCATO ALLA GRIGLIA
Grilled Spatchcocked Chicken

Sometimes I need the scent of live fire on my chicken. Or it's too hot in the middle of the summer—or too beautiful outside—to think about turning on the oven in our kitchen. The grill is the answer. This split-open, seasoned, and basted bird has that balance of char and juicy meat that will have your guests licking their fingers and going back for seconds.

SERVES 4

1 (4- to 6-lb/1.8- to 2.7-kg) whole chicken

Kosher or coarse sea salt

Freshly ground black pepper

1 garlic clove, minced

1 sprig rosemary, needles removed and finely chopped

Juice from 1 lemon

½ cup (120 ml) high-quality extra-virgin olive oil

To split and dry brine the chicken:

1. Using a sharp chef's knife, insert the point into the center of the breastbone until it breaks through and then cut decisively through the rest of the breastbone with the entire blade of the knife. (Note: Many spatchcocking instructions call for removal of the backbone rather than cutting through the breastbone, but I find this Italian-style method preferable, as it conserves the backbone, which has great flavor.) Open up the chicken and begin to flatten it out by pressing down firmly with your hands.

2. Place the split chicken skin-side up on your work surface and cover with a sheet of plastic wrap. Using a meat pounder, mallet, or heavy skillet, pound the chicken all over to make it relatively flat and even. Remove the plastic wrap and season the chicken aggressively on both sides with salt. Put the seasoned bird on a rack placed in a sheet pan and refrigerate, uncovered, for at least 2 hours or up to 24 hours. Remove from the fridge at least 1 hour before you plan to grill to bring the chicken to room temperature.

To cook the chicken:

3. Light a wood or charcoal fire in an outdoor grill or preheat a gas grill.

4. In a small bowl, combine 2 pinches of salt, a few grinds of black pepper, and the garlic, rosemary, lemon juice, and olive oil. Whisk vigorously to create an emulsified mixture. Taste for seasoning, adjust as necessary, and set aside.

5. When your wood or charcoal fire has burned down to glowing embers, you're ready to cook. If using a gas grill, decrease the heat to medium-low. Place the split-open chicken on the grill directly over the flames, skin-side down.

—continued—

POLLO SPACCATO ALLA GRIGLIA
(continued)

6. Grill for about 15 minutes or until the skin has developed a nice golden crust and some char marks. Resist the temptation to touch or fiddle with the bird during the first 4 to 5 minutes of grilling; you'll risk tearing the surface of the bird if you try to move it too soon. Go slowly with the cooking. You want to gradually develop the initial crust on the skin side of the chicken. If your fire is too hot and the skin begins to burn or char too quickly, move the chicken to a cooler part of the grill where it can cook more slowly.

7. Flip the bird over and cook for an additional 10 minutes. Baste the skin—which should now have a nice golden crust and some char marks—with the lemon juice mixture. Continue to cook for another 5 minutes.

8. Flip the chicken back to the skin-side-down position. Baste the bone side with the lemon juice mixture and continue to cook for another 5 to 7 minutes. Flip the bird one more time, baste the skin side again, and finish cooking, another 5 to 7 minutes, depending on the size of your chicken and the heat of your grill. Total cooking time, from start to finish, should be 45 to 50 minutes. You'll know the chicken is ready if it sags slightly when picked up with tongs at the backbone. It will almost be ready to break under its own weight. You can also pierce the chicken with the tip of a sharp knife at the joint between one of the drumsticks/thighs; if the juices run clear, the chicken is fully cooked through.

9. Remove the finished chicken from the grill and allow to rest for 10 minutes on a cutting board. After resting, carve the chicken into individual pieces and baste the finished chicken one last time with the lemon juice mixture. Serve family-style on a large warmed platter.

Wine Pairing: Castell' in Villa Chianti Classico Riserva DOCG 2016. Principessa Coralia Pignatelli—now well into her eighties—has produced wine at Castell' in Villa since the early 1970s. These are benchmark Chianti Classico wines. They reflect the special terroir from which they come and the steady guiding hand of the princess. This riserva 2016 stands right up to, and at the same time complements, the Tuscan oak over which this chicken is grilled.

GAIOLESI FRIENDS COME TO AMERICA

A number of years back, we had Gaiolesi friends visit us in the U.S. It was their first time in the U.S., and they told us up front, "We don't want to eat Italian food. Introduce us to typical foods that Americans like to eat." Now, my reaction was twofold. Of course they don't want to eat Italian food—they don't believe it will be any good! On the other hand, I knew there was a sincere adventurousness behind their request, and we were happy to oblige.

One afternoon, after a morning of white water rafting on the Roaring Fork River, we stopped at a local bar in nearby Basalt for lunch. Among lots of other typical pub fare on the menu were Buffalo chicken wings that could be ordered in varying degrees of spiciness: mild, medium, hot, "wise guy," and "catatonic." My friend Luciano, who loves pretty much anything and everything "piccante" and is never one to shy away from a challenge, ordered the "catatonic," despite my advice not to. Though I could see beads of sweat dripping down his forehead, he loved every bite.

Now, whenever we return to Gaiole after a few months' absence, I inevitably get a nudge from my friend: "Ma John, puoi fare quelle ali di pollo catatoniche? (Can you make those catatonic chicken wings?)" I always oblige, albeit with a lesser degree of heat.

Frank's RedHot Sauce—unavailable as far as I know in Italy—is an indispensable ingredient and is, accordingly, packed in my luggage regularly.

ALI DI POLLO "CATATONICHE"
Spicy Buffalo-Style Chicken Wings

I grill rather than deep-fry these wings. It's easier, less messy, and (somewhat) healthier. And the result is surprisingly close to the traditional deep-fried version.

**SERVES 4 AS A
HEARTY APPETIZER**

12 chicken wing "drumettes"

12 chicken wing "flats," preferably
    with tips attached

Kosher or coarse sea salt

½ cup (115 g) butter

½ cup (120 ml) Frank's RedHot Sauce

6 celery stalks (optional)

Blue cheese dressing (optional)

1. Light a charcoal or wood fire in a grill or preheat a gas grill.

2. Season the chicken wing pieces with salt, but use a restrained hand here. The Buffalo sauce will also add saltiness to the finished wings.

3. Melt the butter slowly in a small saucepan over medium-low heat. When the butter has melted, add the hot sauce and stir to combine well. When the sauce is warmed through, turn off the heat and leave on the stove.

4. Grill the chicken wing pieces over medium heat. Initially, leave the pieces alone without trying to move them until the first side develops some caramelization and they can be turned without sticking to the grill, 7 to 8 minutes. Continue cooking, turning the pieces frequently, until cooked through thoroughly, about 20 minutes of total cooking time. The beauty of chicken wings is that you almost can't overcook them, as long as you're working with low to medium heat. So err on the side of more cooking. An undercooked chicken wing is not a pleasant experience.

5. When the chicken wings have been cooked, put them into a large plastic container big enough to hold them comfortably (or work in batches). It's best to use a plastic food storage container with a tight-sealing lid. Toss the hot sauce mixture over the top of the wings, close the container with the lid, and shake vigorously to thoroughly coat the wings with the sauce. Serve piping hot on a family-style platter with celery stalks and blue cheese dressing on the side for dipping, if desired.

SYRACUSE

My grandparents on both sides were Italian. My mother's family had immigrated to Syracuse, New York, from the province of Campobasso in the region of Molise in the 1920s. Similarly, my paternal grandfather and his brother left the small hilltop town of Sonnino, in the province of Latina, region of Lazio, to join other family members in Syracuse.

In the 1930s and 1940s, the north side of Syracuse was a bustling, almost exclusively Italian enclave with a large immigrant population hailing from Campobasso and the Lazio provinces of Latina and Frosinone. As described by my parents and grandparents, the neighborhood was a reflection of life back in Italy. Small specialty food shops, bakeries, butchers, and restaurants lined the streets. It was a place where everyone knew your name and where the familiar smells and sounds (Italian was still the neighborhood's primary language, at least for the first generation of transplants) of the homeland could be found. These immigrants had fled abject poverty and a hard way of life in Italy and they often chose never to return there. But Italian traditions—those connected with community, church, family, and, of course, food—endured.

As these "North Siders" assimilated and prospered in their new homeland, they eventually "immigrated" again—this time to the suburbs. Better schools, a bigger yard, and modern home amenities were the draw. But the traditions lived on.

My mother's parents lived next door to us in a quintessential *Wonder Years* suburban neighborhood. Growing up, my brother and I spent almost as much time at my grandparents' house as we did at our own.

My grandparents were both wonderful cooks. Their house was always filled with the aroma of one mouthwatering dish or another, and their dining room hosted memorably large gatherings of family and friends, especially during the holidays. As a young boy, I was fascinated by my grandmother's deft hands and graceful way with fresh pasta dough and by the slow, bubbling alchemy of my grandfather's Sunday sauce—a variation of what Neapolitans call "La Genovese." They made it all look easy, natural. There was no stress in the preparation of these simple, gutsy dishes, just lots of attention to detail and, even if it sounds cliché, lots of love.

By the time I was in college, I was regularly cooking for myself and my friends. My repertoire? A slowly growing and evolving collection of Italian-American classics that had defined my childhood. I've continued to expand and revisit this group of dishes ever since.

No, these are not authentic regional Italian dishes that you would find in Tuscany, Lazio, or Molise. Indeed, many American tourists, including Italian-Americans who view themselves as "100 Percent Made in Italy," are disappointed when they discover that chicken parm is not on the list of daily specials at the local trattoria near their hotel. But these dishes do reflect Italian ingenuity and soul. My grandparents, like so many other Italian immigrants to the U.S., learned to make do with what they had, constrained as they were by both a lack of certain Mediterranean ingredients and the financial challenges presented by a new country, new jobs, the Great Depression, and World War II. Despite all of that, they always managed to put something delicious on their dinner table.

I still crave these dishes today. And guess what? I've introduced Italian friends to some of these dishes to rave reviews. Here are a few favorites.

GRILLED PORK CHOPS WITH VINEGAR PEPPERS

Although you may stumble upon a version of vinegar peppers in certain parts of Italy, I think of them as an Italian-American mainstay. And if you do see them in Italy, they'd never be a "top-dressing" for grilled pork chops as they are in this red-checkered-tablecloth-joint classic. You can use bone-in chops from the loin or steaks cut from a pork shoulder.

SERVES 4

2 red bell peppers

1 yellow bell pepper

1 green bell pepper

½ cup (120 ml) high-quality extra-virgin olive oil, plus more as needed

1 garlic clove, crushed

Kosher or coarse sea salt and freshly ground black pepper

3 tablespoons (45 ml) white wine vinegar

4 (1½-inch/3.8-cm-thick) pork chops

Juice of 1 lemon, plus more as needed

1 teaspoon (5 g) honey

1. Stem and seed the peppers and cut them into 1-inch (2.5-cm) wide by 2-inch (5-cm) long strips.

2. In a large sauté pan, heat the olive oil and garlic over low heat. When the garlic begins to take on a golden color, add the peppers and stir well to evenly coat the peppers in the oil. Raise the heat a bit to medium-low. Season the peppers with salt and pepper, stir well, and cook until the peppers begin to soften, about 5 minutes.

3. Add 2 to 3 tablespoons (30 to 45 ml) of water to the sauté pan, lower the heat, and continue cooking the peppers at a low simmer, stirring occasionally, until they are soft but not breaking apart. Turn off the heat and taste for seasoning, adjusting with additional salt and pepper, if necessary. Add the white wine vinegar and stir well to combine. Allow the peppers to cool. They are best served at room temperature.

4. Light a charcoal or wood fire in a grill or preheat a gas grill. You could also use a stovetop grill pan over medium-high heat.

5. Season the pork chops generously on both sides with salt and pepper.

6. In a small bowl, combine the lemon juice and honey and stir well until the honey has dissolved.

—continued—

GRILLED PORK CHOPS WITH VINEGAR PEPPERS *(continued)*

7. When the fire is ready, grill the pork chops directly over medium-high heat. Grill for 2 to 3 minutes without disturbing them to allow the chops to develop enough of a crust on the first side that they can be easily flipped without sticking. Flip the chops and baste them with the lemon/honey mixture (this will help develop additional caramelization on the surface of the chops). Grill for about 2 minutes and flip the chops again. Baste the second side of the chops with the lemon/honey mixture. Cook for about 1 minute or so, and then flip the chops again. (Once a crust has initially developed on the surface of the chops, it's okay, and in fact it's best, to flip often for even cooking and to make sure that the surface of the chops does not burn due to the sugar content of the honey. You want beautiful char/caramelization, but not a burnt result.)

8. When the chops feel firm to the touch when poked with your finger, they are done. They should be cooked through with just a hint of pink at the center. Remove from the grill and allow the chops to rest on a warmed platter for at least 5 minutes.

9. Place one chop on each of four plates, drizzle with olive oil, squeeze a bit of lemon juice on top of each chop, and top them with a generous portion of the vinegar peppers. Serve immediately.

Wine Pairing: Cupano Brunello di Montalcino DOCG 2015. The Cupano wines walk the fine line between traditional and more modern-style Brunello, and they do so with elegance and finesse.

CHICKEN PIZZAIOLO

The "pizzaiolo" style, which can be applied to chicken, beef, pork, or even certain fish (minus the cheese), traces its origin back to the Italian-American tradition of topping a protein with a sauce and melted cheese in the style of a pizza. The sauce consists of one or more of sautéed peppers, mushrooms, and onions, plus a touch of simple tomato sauce. In this version, I use all three with melted mozzarella cheese to bring back the memory of a dish served at Grimaldi's Ristorante in Syracuse, New York, circa 1972.

SERVES 4

1 red bell pepper

1 yellow bell pepper

1½ cups (360 ml) high-quality extra-virgin olive oil, plus more as needed

1 garlic clove, crushed

1 small yellow onion, diced

Kosher or coarse sea salt and freshly ground black pepper

6 ounces (170 g) cremini or portobello mushrooms, cut into bite-size pieces

4 boneless, skinless chicken breasts

All-purpose flour

1 cup (240 ml) Basic Tomato Sauce (page 105)

8 slices fresh cow's milk mozzarella (sometimes called "fior' di latte")

8 fresh basil leaves

1 lemon

1. Stem and seed the peppers and cut them into 1-inch (2.5-cm) wide by 2-inch (5-cm) long strips.

2. In a large sauté pan, heat ½ cup (120 ml) of the olive oil and the garlic over low heat. When the garlic begins to take on a golden color, add the peppers and onions and stir well to evenly coat everything in the oil. Raise the heat a bit to medium-low. Season with salt and pepper, stir well, and cook until the peppers begin to soften, about 5 minutes.

3. Add 2 to 3 tablespoons (30 to 45 ml) of water to the sauté pan, lower the heat, and continue cooking the peppers and onions at a low simmer, stirring occasionally, until they are soft but not breaking apart. Turn off the heat and taste for seasoning, adjusting with additional salt and pepper, if necessary. Set aside and allow the peppers to cool.

4. Heat ½ cup (120 ml) of olive oil in a sauté pan over medium heat. When the oil is shimmering, add the mushrooms, season with salt and pepper, and stir to combine them with the oil. At first, the mushrooms will absorb almost all the oil. As the cooking progresses, the mushrooms will release the oil as they lose their moisture and they will begin to take on a nice golden color and caramelization, 5 to 7 minutes. Taste for seasoning, adjust as necessary, and set the mushrooms aside.

5. Carefully cut each chicken breast in half horizontally to create 8 total pieces, each half as thick as the intact breast piece. Working in batches of 2 at a time, place the sliced chicken pieces in a large plastic zip-top bag (no need to seal it) or under a sheet of plastic wrap. Pound the pieces lightly with a meat pounder, mallet, or heavy pan to create thin, even pieces.

—continued—

CHICKEN PIZZAIOLO
(continued)

6. Season the chicken pieces with salt and pepper, then sprinkle them lightly on both sides with flour. Shake each piece to remove any excess flour.

7. Heat the remaining ½ cup (120 ml) of olive oil in a heavy-bottomed sauté pan or cast-iron skillet over medium-high heat. When the oil is shimmering, add a few of the chicken pieces, being careful not to overcrowd the pan. Cook the first side of the chicken pieces until a light golden/caramelized color is developed. Flip the pieces and cook the second side until golden. Set aside.

8. Continue working in batches until all the pieces have been sautéed. (Don't worry if it appears that the chicken is not cooked completely through. The final cooking will occur in the pizzaiolo sauce; this initial step is only to caramelize the chicken pieces and to leave some brown bits on the bottom of the pan to add additional flavor and complexity to the finished sauce.)

9. When all the chicken pieces have been sautéed and set aside, remove the pan from the heat and discard any excess oil. Place the pan back over medium heat and drizzle the pan with 2 to 3 tablespoons (30 to 45 ml) of olive oil. When the pan has heated back up, add the pepper/onion mixture and the sautéed mushrooms and mix well. When the vegetables start to sizzle, add just enough water to the pan to cover the bottom. Deglaze the pan, scraping up the caramelized bits on the bottom with a wooden spoon and mixing everything well.

10. Add just enough of the tomato sauce to the pan to give the sauce a hint of red color. Stir well to combine and lower the heat to maintain a bare simmer.

11. Slip the sautéed chicken pieces into the simmering sauce, turning each piece over once or twice to coat them well. Simmer the chicken in the bubbling sauce for 3 to 4 minutes to ensure they are cooked through. If the sauce seems to be thickening too much, add a bit more water to the pan as needed.

12. Place a slice of fresh mozzarella and a fresh basil leaf on top of each chicken piece. Cover the pan and continue to cook until the cheese is oozing. Remove from the heat and drizzle with a bit more olive oil and a few spritzes of fresh lemon juice. Bring to the table and serve family-style.

Wine Pairing: Maurizio Alongi Chianti Classico Riserva DOCG "Vigna Barbischio" 2019. A beautiful expression of Chianti, produced high above Gaiole in nearby Barbischio, by longtime consulting enologist and now winery owner Maurizio Alongi.

RIGATONI ALLA VODKA (NEL MODO DI CARBONE)
Rigatoni alla Vodka Carbone-Style

The classic rigatoni alla vodka on Italian-American menus always intrigued me as a young boy. There seemed to be something taboo about it . . . was there really vodka in that dish? Could I order it at twelve years old? Would it make me tipsy? Years later, I was not surprised to learn that there is no vodka in rigatoni alla vodka.

At Carbone, in New York City, this dish has developed a cult following, and rightfully so. The Carbone version features house-made rigatoni with a spicy, slightly acidic pink sauce that piques your taste buds and holds your attention bite after bite. I've experimented on my own to try to replicate Carbone's "holy grail." My version uses high-quality dried rigatoni in place of the fresh-made (impossible to make properly without an expensive bronze die pasta extruder). The spicy kick is provided by preserved Calabrian chile peppers and is balanced by the sweetness of the slow-cooked shallots and the cream that takes the sauce from red to pink.

SERVES 4

Kosher or coarse sea salt

1 tablespoon (15 g) butter

4 medium shallots, thinly sliced

1 pound (455 g) high-quality dried rigatoni (preferably Afeltra or Mancini brand)

1 tablespoon (15 ml) high-quality extra-virgin olive oil, plus more as needed

2 cups (480 g) Basic Tomato Sauce (page 105)

1 tablespoon (12 g) chopped preserved Calabrian chile peppers

1 cup (240 ml) heavy cream

Parmigiano-Reggiano cheese

1. Bring a large pot of salted water to a rolling boil over high heat.

2. In a small pot or sauté pan, melt the butter over low heat. Add the shallots together with just enough water to cover the shallots. Cook until the water has completely evaporated and the shallots have completely softened, but not browned, 8 to 10 minutes. Set aside.

3. Toss the rigatoni into the boiling water and cook until al dente (see Some Thoughts on Pasta, page 36).

4. While the pasta is cooking, prepare the sauce. In a large sauté pan, heat the olive oil over low heat. Add the softened shallots, stir to combine, and immediately add the tomato sauce and Calabrian chile peppers. Increase the heat to medium, bring to a light simmer, and stir well to combine. Slowly add some of the heavy cream to the sauce until you reach the "pinkness" that appeals to you. Some people prefer this dish on the red side; others—like me—like it more toward the pink. Stir well to combine and simmer for 1 or 2 minutes. Set aside.

5. Use a strainer to transfer the pasta to the pan with the sauce and heat over medium-low heat, stirring well to combine. If necessary, add a spoonful or two of the pasta cooking water to create an even, balanced emulsion of sauce and pasta, while stirring constantly. When you've achieved the desired consistency, turn off the heat, drizzle the pasta with some olive oil, scatter a generous amount of Parmigiano-Reggiano over the top, and stir once more to amalgamate and incorporate everything together. Serve immediately in warmed bowls with extra Parmigiano-Reggiano on the side.

INSALATA DI CESARE
Classic Caesar Salad

I'm not sure whether Caesar salad should be cataloged as part of the Italian-American culinary repertoire or whether it's more commonly associated with the great tradition of American steakhouses. Either way, this is a dish that I love.

Years ago, I was traveling for business and decided to have dinner in the hotel restaurant. Caesar salad was on the menu. The dining room captain rolled a cart up alongside my table and began an elaborate tableside preparation in the old-school tradition. I was fascinated by his confident, decisive motions as he emulsified the dressing in a well-seasoned wooden serving bowl. The resulting salad was delicious. I decided then and there that this was one of those "renaissance man skills" that I needed to acquire.

I can think of very few dishes that pack the same level of umami punch as a well-made Caesar salad. In my version, anchovies, Worcestershire sauce, soy sauce, mustard, and Parmigiano-Reggiano combine for a super-umami explosion.

SERVES 4

2 salt-packed anchovies, well rinsed, bones removed, and finely chopped

3 or 4 garlic cloves, finely minced

2 tablespoons (30 ml) Dijon mustard

2 tablespoons (30 ml) soy sauce

2 tablespoons (30 ml) Worcestershire sauce

2 or 3 dashes Tabasco sauce

1 egg yolk

Juice of 1 lemon

⅓ cup (80 ml) white wine vinegar

1 cup (100 g) grated Parmigiano-Reggiano cheese

Freshly ground black pepper

½ cup (120 ml) high-quality extra-virgin olive oil, plus more as needed

1 large head romaine lettuce, washed, dried, and cut into bite-size pieces

1. Combine the anchovies and garlic in a big salad bowl (wooden is best) and mash them up together using a pestle, fork, or the back of a spoon until you achieve a paste-like consistency.

2. Add the mustard, soy sauce, Worcestershire, and Tabasco and whisk together until well incorporated.

3. Add the egg yolk, lemon juice, white wine vinegar, ½ cup (50 g) of the Parmigiano-Reggiano cheese, and a generous amount of freshly ground black pepper. Whisk together to incorporate.

4. Slowly drizzle in olive oil in a steady stream, whisking vigorously until all the ingredients are fully incorporated into a creamy, emulsified consistency. If you have the time, it's best to scoop the dressing out of the salad bowl, place it in a covered container, and refrigerate it for at least 30 minutes or up to 3 hours before using. This helps the dressing take on a sturdier body, perfect for mixing the salad.

5. When it's time to mix the salad, start with about half of the dressing on the bottom of the bowl (if you have proceeded directly to mixing the salad without giving the dressing any time in the refrigerator, just scoop about half of it out of the bowl and set it aside); you can always add more if you need it. Toss the romaine lettuce into the bowl. Add the remaining ½ cup (50 g) of Parmigiano-Reggiano and several grinds of fresh ground pepper. Mix everything together thoroughly until the lettuce is well coated, adding more dressing if needed. Serve immediately.

TUSCANY'S DIRTY LITTLE SECRET

The bread in Tuscany is awful. There. I said it. And it's true.

Great bread does exist in other Italian regions. I've had mouthwatering loaves in Rome, beautiful flatbreads and focaccia in Puglia, and dense, chewy sandwich rolls in Milan. But Tuscan bread—setting aside a few exceptions—leaves me cold.

Yes, I've heard all the excuses and rationalizations from my Tuscan friends. "You don't like it because it's unsalted." "It's intentionally bland because our salumi are so highly seasoned and our food is so rich." "It's baked this way so it lasts longer . . . we don't waste anything here." Blah blah blah.

Here's the truth. Tuscan bread, in general, is bad. I cringe when I see American tourists taste this bread for the first time. They smile and nod their heads in approval—after all, this is Italy, and furthermore, this is Tuscany. Of course this is great bread. They want to, and believe they should, love it. I also felt that way back at the beginning of our Tuscan adventure. But you can only fake it for so long.

There are excellent examples of artisanally made bread in Tuscany. But they are few and far between. The lack of salt has nothing to do with the general low quality of bread here—that's a matter of personal taste. A saltless loaf can and should still have great texture and a great crust, which can only be produced by a slowly fermented dough that is properly baked. Unfortunately, and I can't explain why, given the region's passion for all things artisanal, the traditions of great bread making have been lost here. What you are typically served is bread that is tasteless, spongy, and stale.

My solution: We bake our own bread.

Bread making can seem intimidating. And it does take some practice as well as some trial and error to get it right. But it's easier than one might think. And the personal satisfaction of pulling your own handmade loaf from the oven and sinking your teeth into a beautiful slice of dense, chewy, crusty bread is a true pleasure.

There's a lot of bad information out there about bread baking. And there's a lot of good information that is overly complicated and difficult for the average aspiring home baker to follow. And then there is the book that clarified it all for me: *Flour Water Salt Yeast* by Ken Forkish. If you want to get up to speed quickly on how to make great bread at home, buy this book.

Forkish is a longtime artisanal bread baker and pizza maker in Portland, Oregon. He brings a palpable passion for the subject to his writing and a nerdish attention to detail in how he's worked out the mechanics of making good bread at home versus how it's done in a professional bakery. He's done all the hard work for you, including all the experimentation to find the right ratios of those four ingredients as well as the time and temperature that will work with those ingredients to produce a great bread dough. He advocates the use of Dutch ovens to bake bread at home—a technique that mimics a professional bread oven's ability to inject moisture into the baking chamber to produce those crusty, dense loaves we love.

Take the time and make the modest investment in the necessary equipment (a kitchen thermometer, a scale, an appropriate-size Dutch oven, a couple of proofing baskets) to try your hand at homemade loaves. Weigh your ingredients (we've moved from the art of cooking to the science of baking here) and pay close attention to the temperature of the water you use and the room you are working in.

PANE SALATO
Rustic Country-Style Bread

Here's a simplified approach to a "same day" rustic country loaf that follows the Forkish method. When one of these loaves is served at our home, our Tuscan friends will nonchalantly ask, "Dove hai comprato 'sto pane? (Where did you buy this bread?)" I reply with a sly smile, "È un segreto! (It's a secret!)" Note: Quantities are in metric measurements (though I've also provided the U.S. system conversions), which is much easier to ensure proper ratios in baking.

MAKES 2 LOAVES

1 kg (35.3 ounces) high-quality white bread flour (King Arthur produces an excellent bread flour)

720 g (25.4 ounces) water, at 95°F (35°C)

22 g (0.75 ounce) fine sea salt

4 g (about 1 teaspoon) instant dried yeast

To make the dough:

1. In a large bowl, combine the flour and water and mix by hand thoroughly into a shaggy mass. Be sure to incorporate all the flour into the mixture, working with the mass as it forms to pick up any flour on the bottom and sides of the bowl. Cover the bowl tightly with plastic wrap and allow the mass to rest for 20 minutes.

2. Sprinkle the salt and instant dried yeast evenly over the top of the dough mass. Wet your "mixing" hand with warm water, reach under the dough mass, and pull it up over itself in three or four places to enclose the dough mass around the salt and yeast.

3. Wet your mixing hand again. Using your thumb and forefinger as a "pincer," squeeze completely through the dough mass three or four times in a line. After this pinching maneuver, reach under the dough in three or four places, pulling it up and over itself back into a roundish form. Repeat both processes—pinching and then reshaping the dough mass—five or six times, until the yeast and salt have been fully incorporated into the dough mass and the dough begins to feel smooth and homogenous. Cover the bowl tightly with plastic wrap and allow the dough to rest for 30 minutes.

4. Uncover the dough and, with a wet hand, turn the dough over onto itself in three or four places, pulling up from under the dough and closing it back over itself. After those initial turns, reach under the entire mass and flip it over so that the bottom is now facing up. Recover the bowl tightly and allow to rest for 45 minutes.

—continued—

PANE SALATO
(continued)

5. Uncover the dough and repeat the process described in step 4. Recover the bowl tightly with the plastic wrap and place it in a warm part of your kitchen where it will rest for 3 to 4 additional hours, depending on the ambient temperature of the room, until the dough has more than doubled in size and air bubbles are visible in parts of the dough. This signals that the initial fermentation of the dough is complete.

6. Turn the fermented dough out onto a lightly floured work surface. It's best to sprinkle some flour around the perimeter of the dough in the mixing bowl, and then gently work your hands under the entire dough perimeter, reaching under and carefully pulling the dough out of the bowl. Be gentle. You don't want to ruin your work and patience by deflating your dough mass and losing the beautiful gases that have developed within.

7. With floured hands, loosely form the turned-out dough into a rectangular shape. Sprinkle some flour on top of the dough in a line, dividing the dough mass into two roughly equal parts. With a dough scraper, cut the dough mass into two pieces where you've sprinkled the flour. Using the scraper, loosely form each half into a circular mass.

8. With lightly floured hands, shape each circular dough mass into a loaf by gently pulling the sides of each mass out, up, and over itself in three or four places, then inverting the dough mass and gently pulling it toward you with your hands around the mass, turning it a quarter turn at a time, to form a tight ball. You should be able to feel some tension in the dough ball as it stretches against the gases trapped inside.

9. Lightly flour two proofing baskets or round bowls. Place each shaped dough ball in the proofing basket and place each basket inside a plastic bag to cover tightly. Allow the dough balls to proof for 45 to 60 minutes, again depending on the ambient temperature of the room. Check the dough balls after the first 45 minutes by pressing them with a lightly floured finger. If the indentation springs back slowly and incompletely, the dough ball is perfectly proofed and ready for baking. If the indentation springs back immediately and almost completely, the dough is not yet fully proofed and needs more time. If the indentation does not spring back at all, you've probably waited too long and the dough may be overproofed (in which case it may not rise ideally when baked and may lack the complex interior of a perfectly proofed loaf).

To bake the dough

(Note: It's best to complete steps 10 and 11 for preheating while the dough balls are proofing; otherwise, you risk overproofing them as you wait for the oven to come up to temperature so baking can begin):

10. Preheat the oven to 475°F (245°C).

11. Place two covered Dutch ovens on the middle rack of the oven. (If you only have one, you can bake one loaf at a time; simply put the second dough ball in the refrigerator while you bake the first loaf; this will ensure that the second dough ball does not overproof while you bake the first.)

12. Turn the proofed dough balls out onto a lightly floured work surface, flipping the proofing baskets over and lightly tapping them to release the dough balls onto the work surface. What was the bottom of the dough ball in the proofing basket should now be the top of the dough ball on the work surface.

13. With heavy oven mitts, carefully remove the Dutch ovens from the oven and remove the covers. With lightly floured hands, gently reach under each dough ball and transfer it to a Dutch oven, being careful not to touch the hot sides with your bare hands.

14. With the oven mitts back on, recover the Dutch ovens, set them back in the oven, and bake for 30 minutes. Remove the lids. The loaves should show a good amount of "oven-spring," having partially baked and risen during the initial 30 minutes. The color of the loaves should be a light copper tone. Continue baking for an additional 10 to 15 minutes, until the exterior of the loaves is a deep mahogany color, perhaps just a bit longer than you might think. Check the loaves after the first 10 minutes—the heat of your oven will determine whether the loaves are properly browned in more or less time.

15. Turn the fully baked loaves out onto your countertop by tipping the Dutch ovens carefully over the work surface. Turn each loaf on its side against a serving bowl to allow air to circulate freely and completely around each loaf. Cool the loaves thoroughly, for at least 30 minutes and preferably for 1 hour. This cooling allows the loaves to "temper" and develop a crunchy crust and beautiful dense interior.

—continued—

16. With a serrated bread knife, cut the bread into generous slices and serve. The best way to cut the bread is to initially cut a loaf in half. Place the two halves cut-side down, which will give you a stable "platform" for cutting slices to your desired thickness.

Bonus Dish . . . Piatto di Recupero!

If you only make one loaf and have leftover dough, you can store the extra dough in a zip-top plastic bag in the refrigerator. The dough will keep for up to 5 days. It's ideal for a simple focaccia. Take the dough out of the refrigerator about 30 minutes before you plan to bake.

Place the dough in a well-oiled 18-by-26-inch (45-by-66-cm) sheet pan and gently begin to flatten it out to fit the tray, starting from the center and working your way out toward the sides of the pan. Don't rush it; if the dough is resistant at first, let it rest for 10 to 15 minutes and then continue gently flattening and shaping it toward the sides of the pan. Working with a one-loaf quantity of leftover dough, you're likely to have at least 2 inches (5 cm) of space between the edges of the flattened dough and the edges of the sheet pan when you've reached the correct rectangular shape and thickness.

Gently press into the flattened dough all over with your fingertips to create "dimples" on the surface of the dough. Drizzle with olive oil, season lightly with sea salt, and scatter with chopped fresh rosemary (totally optional).

Bake for 5 to 7 minutes in the bottom third of a preheated 450°F (235°C) oven. Check the bottom of the focaccia—it should be firmed up and starting to brown. If not, give it another minute or so. Move the focaccia to the top third of the oven and finish baking, until the top is golden brown and the focaccia is puffed up and cooked through, another 8 to 10 minutes. Remove the finished focaccia from the oven, place it on a rack, and allow to cool for 5 to 7 minutes. Cut and serve warm.

CONTORNI
Side Dishes

A main course dish in a traditional Italian restaurant won't usually include any kind of side vegetable or starch component. Rather, the "contorni," what we'd consider side dishes in the U.S., are separately listed and ordered to accompany the main part of the meal. Here are a few favorites (in addition to those already scattered throughout this book) that might accompany any number of the meat and fish dishes presented here.

BIETOLA O SPINACIO IN PADELLA
Sautéed Swiss Chard or Spinach

Tuscans love greens. All kinds of greens. Most commonly seen on restaurant menus are spinach and chard. But you might also find cicoria (chicory), scarola (escarole), and agretti (a Mediterranean green that looks like a cross between seaweed and long green serpent beans). This simple sauté of greens can be applied to any of these varieties, though for the more bitter or tough cicoria, scarola, and agretti, I'd recommend first a quick blanching in boiling salted water followed by a plunge into an ice bath. This will set the color and soften the greens before sautéing.

SERVES 4 AS A SIDE DISH

3 large bunches fresh Swiss chard or spinach

½ cup (120 ml) high-quality extra-virgin olive oil, plus more as needed

1 garlic clove, cut into 3 or 4 pieces

Kosher or coarse sea salt and freshly ground black pepper

½ lemon

1. Thoroughly wash the greens; there is nothing worse than gritty greens. If the spinach is small, young, and tender, it's perfectly fine to leave the stems on. Otherwise, if you're working with more mature spinach or Swiss chard, it's best to take the time to remove the leaves from the stems—but even that is optional. Chop the greens into bite-size pieces.

2. In a sauté pan large enough to accommodate the greens, heat the olive oil and garlic over medium-low heat. When the garlic is just beginning to brown, add the greens to the pan, season with salt and pepper, raise the heat to medium, and stir everything well to combine.

3. Cook the greens, stirring frequently, until they begin to wilt and give off their liquid. Decrease the heat to low and continue to cook until the greens are thoroughly softened, the liquid in the pan has all but evaporated, and the greens are glistening with olive oil. Turn off the heat and taste for seasoning. Adjust for salt and pepper, if necessary. Squeeze a bit of fresh lemon juice over the greens, drizzle with a bit more olive oil, and stir well to combine.

4. Serve immediately, family-style, in a warmed serving bowl. The greens can be prepared 2 to 3 hours in advance and reheated just before serving.

FAGIOLINI CON AGLIO, CIPOLLETTA, E POMODORINI

Green Beans with Garlic, Scallion, and Cherry Tomatoes

Green beans are abundant at spring and summer markets throughout Chianti. As fresh scallions (cipollette) and cherry tomatoes (pomodorini) make their appearances, this contorno that marries the three becomes a favorite at Casa Bersani.

SERVES 4 AS A SIDE DISH

Kosher or coarse sea salt

1 pound (455 g) fresh green beans, tips removed and thoroughly washed

½ cup (120 ml) high-quality extra-virgin olive oil

1 garlic clove, sliced

12 cherry tomatoes, rinsed and halved

2 scallions, trimmed and finely chopped from their white ends into their soft green parts

Freshly ground black pepper

½ lemon

1. Bring a large pot of water to a boil over high heat. Season the boiling water generously with salt. Prepare an ice water bath in a large bowl or plastic tub.

2. Toss the beans into the boiling water and blanch for about 2 minutes. Remove the beans with a mesh spider and immediately submerge them in the ice bath. When the beans have cooled completely, 3 to 4 minutes, remove them from the water and dry them thoroughly with kitchen towels or paper towels.

3. In a large sauté pan, heat the olive oil and garlic over medium-low heat. Just as the garlic begins to take on some color, add the cherry tomatoes and scallions and stir well to combine. Raise the heat slightly and cook for about 1 minute, until the tomatoes just begin to give off some juices and the scallions have become translucent.

4. Add the green beans to the pan. Season with salt and freshly ground pepper. Stir well to combine the ingredients, lower the heat, and continue to cook for 2 minutes.

5. Add just enough water to barely cover the bottom of the pan, put a cover on the pan, and continue cooking for about 5 more minutes, checking occasionally to make sure the bottom of the pan does not completely dry out.

6. When the beans are soft and completely cooked through (but not wilted), they are done. Turn off the heat, taste for seasoning, and adjust as necessary. Squeeze some fresh lemon juice over the beans, drizzle with a bit more olive oil, and stir one last time to combine.

7. Serve in a warmed serving bowl. The beans can be prepared 2 to 3 hours in advance and reheated just before serving.

CIME DI RAPA SALTATE
Sautéed Broccoli Rabe

Cime di rape—known as broccoli rabe in Italian-American neighborhoods throughout the U.S.—is much more commonly eaten in Southern Italy. The regional cuisines of Campania, Basilicata, and Puglia all have their favored preparations and, in some cases, even their own names for this delicious bitter green.

Here is my take on a simple side dish preparation with just a bit of a spicy kick from Calabrian chile pepper and an imperceptible touch of honey that balances out the green's sometimes harsh bitterness.

SERVES 6 AS A SIDE DISH

Kosher or coarse sea salt

3 or 4 bunches broccoli rabe, thoroughly washed and tough stems cut off

½ cup (120 ml) high-quality extra-virgin olive oil

2 garlic cloves, sliced

2 teaspoons (8 g) chopped preserved Calabrian chile pepper

Freshly ground black pepper

Drizzle of artisanal honey

½ lemon

1. Bring a large pot of water to a boil over high heat. Season the water generously with salt. Prepare an ice water bath in a large bowl.

2. Toss the broccoli rabe into the boiling water and blanch for about 1 minute; you don't want to fully cook the broccoli rabe but rather set its green color. You'll finish the cooking later as a slow braise.

3. Remove the broccoli rabe from the boiling water with a mesh spider and immediately submerge it in the ice bath. When the broccoli rabe has cooled completely, 3 to 4 minutes, remove it from the water, then squeeze out and dry it as best you can with kitchen towels or paper towels. A little residual water is okay.

4. In a large sauté pan, heat the olive oil and garlic over medium-low heat. Just as the garlic begins to take on some color, add the broccoli rabe and the Calabrian chile pepper. Season with salt and freshly ground pepper and stir well to combine. Raise the heat slightly and cook the broccoli rabe for about 2 minutes to get the cooking process started.

5. Add just enough water to cover the bottom of the pan by about ½ inch (1.3 cm). Place a cover loosely on the pan and lower the heat to maintain a bare simmer. Continue cooking at a low simmer for 8 to 10 more minutes, checking occasionally to make sure the bottom of the pan does not completely dry out.

6. When the broccoli rabe is soft and completely cooked through (but not breaking apart), it's done. Turn off the heat, taste for seasoning, and adjust as necessary. Drizzle a bit of honey over the broccoli rabe (just a bit; you don't want to notice the sweetness in the final dish, but instead are looking for the balance the honey gives to the bitterness of the greens). Squeeze some fresh lemon juice over the broccoli rabe, drizzle with a bit more olive oil, and stir one last time to combine.

7. Serve family-style in a warmed bowl. The broccoli rabe can be prepared 2 to 3 hours in advance and reheated just before serving.

ZUCCHINE GRATINATE
Zucchini Gratin

The "gratinato" method can be applied to lots of different vegetables and even some fish and chicken dishes. The essence of the technique is to take a close-to-finished dish, embellish it with a shower of freshly grated Parmigiano, add some toasted bread crumbs, and give it all a quick trip into a hot oven. The final result is seductively cheesy and crunchy. I like to give zucchini this treatment—even in midsummer—just to change things up and make what can become routine something unexpected and special.

SERVES 4 AS A SIDE DISH

Kosher or coarse sea salt

6 to 8 fresh zucchini, rinsed and cut into ½-inch (1.3-cm) thick rounds

½ cup (120 ml) high-quality extra-virgin olive oil, plus more as needed

½ cup (120 ml) Basic Tomato Sauce (page 105)

1 cup (100 g) grated Parmigiano-Reggiano cheese

2 sprigs thyme

Freshly ground black pepper

½ cup (50 g) toasted bread crumbs (optional)

1. Salt the zucchini slices on both sides. In a colander set over a bowl, place the zucchini slices in layers separated by paper towels. Place a heavy object (canned tomatoes or a heavy pan) on top of the zucchini and allow to sit for about 30 minutes. This procedure will extract much of the water from the zucchini and make them easier to work with.

2. Pat the zucchini dry with paper towels or kitchen towels.

3. Heat the olive oil in a large sauté pan over medium-high heat. Working in batches to avoid overcrowding the pan, sauté the zucchini slices on both sides until they begin to take on some color. Remove and place in a single layer on paper towels to absorb excess olive oil. Allow to cool to room temperature.

4. Preheat the oven to 450°F (235°C).

5. In an ovenproof casserole large enough to accommodate the zucchini in two or three layers, spread enough of the tomato sauce on the bottom of the casserole to cover it, followed by a layer of zucchini, a generous sprinkling of Parmigiano-Reggiano, and a sprig of thyme. Repeat this layering at least one more time, preferably twice, finishing with cheese on top, a few grinds of freshly ground pepper, and the toasted bread crumbs, if using. Drizzle a bit more olive oil on top and cover tightly with aluminum foil.

6. Place on the center rack of the oven and bake for 20 to 25 minutes, until it is bubbling under the foil. Remove the foil and continue to bake for another 5 to 7 minutes, until the top is brown and caramelized. Remove from the oven, let cool for at least 10 minutes, and serve.

INSALATINA DI CARCIOFI E PARMIGIANO
Baby Artichoke and Parmigiano-Reggiano Salad

Sometimes I need a bright, fresh burst of flavor to jump-start my meal. A simple salad—an insalatina—dressed with lemon juice and extra-virgin olive oil does the trick. Depending on the season, I might use baby artichokes, as in this recipe, or zucchini as a foil against the umami hit of Parmigiano-Reggiano cheese. It's all about balance and simplicity. The grassiness of the artichokes, the acidity of the lemon juice, the peppery hit of good extra-virgin olive oil, and the deep bass notes of the cheese are a great way to wake up your taste buds for the dishes to follow.

SERVES 4

1 lemon, cut in half

6 to 8 baby artichokes, trimmed and tough outer leaves removed

Parmigiano-Reggiano cheese

4 or 5 basil leaves, torn into small pieces

Coarse sea or kosher salt and freshly ground black pepper

High-quality extra-virgin olive oil

1. Pour water into a bowl and add a squeeze of lemon juice. This acidulated water will prevent the artichokes from browning. Thinly slice the artichokes (best achieved on a mandoline-style slicer, but it can be done by hand with a sharp knife) and immediately place them in the acidulated water.

2. When ready to assemble the salad, remove the artichoke slices from the water and dry them thoroughly on paper towels.

3. With a vegetable peeler, shave 10 to 12 ribbons of Parmigiano.

4. On a family-style serving platter, spread out the artichoke slices and top evenly with the ribbons of Parmigiano. Strew the basil pieces over the top.

5. Season the salad ingredients with salt (a restrained hand is required here; the Parmigiano will provide a lot of the needed seasoning on its own) and pepper. Drizzle generously with olive oil and squeeze some lemon juice over the top as a last touch. Serve immediately.

INSALATINA DI FINOCCHIO ED ARANCE SANGUIGNE
Fennel and Blood Orange Salad

When fennel is in season, this starter salad is another first-rate palate awakener. I love the interplay between the licorice undertone of the fennel and the bright citrus hit of the blood oranges.

SERVES 4

2 large fennel bulbs, feathery ends removed and set aside

1 large blood orange, peeled and cut into bite-size pieces, seeds removed

Coarse sea or kosher salt and freshly ground black pepper

High-quality extra-virgin olive oil

1. Remove the tough core from the fennel bulbs. With a mandoline or sharp knife, cut each bulb into thin slices and scatter on a large family-style serving tray.

2. Scatter the pieces of blood orange on top of the fennel slices.

3. Season generously with salt and pepper. Drizzle generously with olive oil. Serve immediately.

PICCOLO DISCORSO DEL VINO
A Few Thoughts on Wine . . .

For me, there are few pleasures greater than drinking a finely crafted Chianti or Brunello in a local trattoria within a twenty-minute drive of its provenance. The best wines—those produced by artisans with dirt under their fingernails and a reverence for the terroir rather than manipulative cellar practices—are living expressions of this beautiful land. Every time I open a bottle, whether an everyday table wine or a special-occasion rarity, I think of the many hands it took to bring that wine to life, the way that mother nature stepped in for a given vintage with challenges or blessings, and the happy coincidence of variables—some controllable, others not—that combined in a particular way to mark the wine with its own unique personality.

You may not be able to make it to Chianti to drink a special bottle "in sito." But thanks to the miracle of worldwide distribution chains, you can bring a slice of Tuscan soul in a bottle to your dining table. Paired with the right food, a good wine can transport you, at least spiritually, to its origins. In Italy, a meal without at least one glass of good wine is an incomplete meal. Food brings out the best in an Italian wine, and, conversely, a good wine brings out the best in a meal.

The personal wine suggestions and pairings throughout this book are just a nudge to get you interested and set you on your own path of wine discovery. At the end of the day, it's really a matter of personal taste and preference. Find what you like and enjoy it. Visit a well-stocked local wine shop and seek advice and opinions from the staff. In my experience, wine professionals are some of the most open, welcoming, and passionate people on the planet. They want to share their knowledge without airs and without judgment. Find your own personal guide to help you sort through the seemingly infinite choices and to cut through the wine-geek jargon that dominates wine labeling and professional reviews.

The subject of Tuscan wine and my own personal journey with it would require the writing of another book. For now, I'll limit myself to noting a few key things about these wines that may help spark your own Tuscan wine love affair.

THE PLACES
In my humble opinion, wine is first and foremost about place. It's the special combination of climate, soil, and topography that imparts personality and uniqueness to great wine regions. Nowhere is this any more apparent than in Tuscany.

At the risk of oversimplification—there are so many variables and microclimates within any given region—I would carve Tuscany up into four major winemaking areas: Chianti Classico/Chianti and the immediately surrounding areas; Montalcino; Montepulciano; and coastal Tuscany. A strong argument could be made for adding the winemaking subregion near the city of Cortona, where recent winemaking successes with international grape varieties, especially Syrah, have drawn much attention.

THE GRAPES
Every great wine region has its bedrock indigenous grape varieties. When we think of Bordeaux, we

naturally think of Cabernet Sauvignon and Merlot. Burgundy conjures thoughts of Chardonnay and Pinot Noir, while the great wines of the Italian northwest (think Barolo and Barbaresco) are made from the Nebbiolo grape.

Tuscany is the land of Sangiovese. Though nonindigenous international grape varietals have taken on more prominence throughout Tuscany, especially in the past forty-five years as so-called Super Tuscan wines became a sensation, Sangiovese remains the backbone of Tuscan wine. The grape does not do well anywhere else in the world, making its connection to place that much stronger.

THE WINES

Italian wine labeling can be confusing. As opposed to the straightforward marketing and labeling of American wines (a Cabernet is a Cabernet; a Chardonnay is a Chardonnay . . .), newcomers to Italian wine may be baffled or misled by names like Chianti, Vino Nobile, and Brunello, not to mention "Super Tuscan."

For the most part, Chianti and Vino Nobile wines (Vino Nobile wines are those produced in the Montepulciano subregion) are Sangiovese-dominated blends. Traditional producers add indigenous blending grapes such as canaiolo or colorino to complement the Sangiovese, while others opt for international varieties like Merlot to round out and soften their wines. Just to confuse things, some Chiantis are 100 percent Sangiovese, with no blending at all.

By law and regulation, Brunello di Montalcino—inarguably one of the world's great wines—must be 100 percent Sangiovese. These wines, made from a Sangiovese clone known generically as Sangiovese Grosso, offer more complexity and more aging potential than the wines of Chianti or Montepulciano, and would generally be enjoyed by

Tuscans on special occasions and to accompany special meals.

Finally, we have the so-called Super Tuscans. These popular—and in some cases cultlike—wines originated as Bordeaux-style blends of Cabernet, Merlot, Cabernet Franc, and Petit Verdot from the Tuscan coast, where favorable maritime conditions are kind to these international varietals. But, with the passage of time, other Tuscan winemakers took note of the public relations success of the "Super Tuscan" label, and many other wines from all over Tuscany adopted Super Tuscan marketing. Today, many wines from Chianti, Montalcino, Montepulciano, and other subregions are marketed and sold as Super Tuscans. These wines could be almost anything, from 100 percent Sangiovese to Chianti-like blends to 100 percent international varietals.

Throughout this book, I've offered some personal thoughts and preferences on wine pairings intended to bring out the best in certain dishes. If you can't find a recommended wine, go with something similar—close geographically or similar in blend or style. Perhaps your local wine guru will have ideas. In any event, do indulge in a glass or two with your meal, and do enjoy the wine journey.

SEASONAL MENUS

As I've said many times throughout this book, let your imagination be your guide in the kitchen. Try to pair dishes together that seem to naturally complement one another, but in the end follow your own instincts, likes, and dislikes. There are no hard-and-fast rules. That said, do try to think about and respect seasonality in what you choose to prepare. It's been said a thousand times before, but it's worth repeating: tomatoes are not very good in December. So maybe don't plan on a caprese salad around the holidays. It'll be way better in August.

Here are a few ideas for meal pairings and seasonality. No stricture here, just some thoughts based on personal experience and preference. As you continue to experiment with the recipes in the book, you'll soon develop your own sense of what works and what doesn't, what you like and what you don't. Enjoy the journey.

PRIMAVERA / SPRING

There's a reawakening of the senses as the countryside sheds its blanket of wintry brown, and green shoots push up in the vineyards and along country roads. If you take it all in the slow way, walking or cycling these sleepy byways, chances are very good you'll cross paths with a crocus or two. Early spring rains set perfect conditions on forest floors for wild mushrooms to sprout. And the season's first produce—peas, asparagus, and favas—take center stage at local markets.

Antipasto: Baccelli freschi e pecorino (page 75)— *Fresh Fava Beans with Pecorino Cheese*

Primo: Tagliatelle ai funghi porcini (page 33)— *Tagliatelle with Porcini Mushrooms*

Secondo: Cacciucco (page 176) con fett'unta (page 182)—*Tuscan Fish Stew with Grilled Country Bread*

ESTATE / SUMMER

By mid-June, the vineyards are a blanket of verdant green and a sea of olive trees stretches on in wave after wave to reflect a silvery light that's hard to describe. The midday heat is intense. Home vegetable gardens are beginning to provide their early bounty and showing signs of what's to come. Fruits and vegetables from the south, where harvest is already in full swing, show up in market stalls.

When the sun goes down and light breezes provide relief from the day's oppressive heat, you can comfortably light the outdoor grill and enjoy an evening of al fresco dining under a blanket of stars.

I like the freshness of the salad that starts this meal followed by the summery clams and spaghetti. The grilled chicken is like an old friend who visits every season; you welcome him back to your table again and again.

Antipasto: Insalatina di finocchio ed arance sanguigne (page 245)—*Fennel and Blood Orange Salad*

Primo: Spaghetti alle vongole (page 102)— *Spaghetti with Clams, White Wine, and Garlic*

Secondo: Pollo spaccato alla griglia (page 215) con peperonata (page 156)—*Grilled Spatchcocked Chicken with Braised Sweet Peppers and Onions*

AUTUNNO / AUTUMN

The smell of fermenting grapes is in the air as nearby wineries begin to crush their fruit and give birth to the year's new wine. The olive trees in our yard are heavy with emerald-green fruit. And the morning air is brisk enough to justify the season's first fire in our family room.

By November, hunting season is in full swing and I'm awakened early on weekend mornings by the crackle of shotguns in the surrounding forests. Teams of hunters flush out wild boar, field dress it, and bring their haul home.

It's time for hearty dishes and the season's last gasp of outdoor cooking.

Antipasto: Antipasto misto "Basilicata Coast-to-Coast" (page 42)—*Mixed Antipasto "Basilicata Coast-to-Coast"*

Primo: Pappardelle al cinghiale (page 151)—*Pappardelle with Wild Boar Sauce*

Secondo: Rosticciane e salsicce alla griglia (page 153) con patate arrosto (page 200) e bietola o spinacio in padella (page 240)—*Grilled Pork Ribs and Sausages with Oven-Roasted Potatoes and Sautéed Swiss Chard*

INVERNO / WINTER

The early rains have started, providing needed resupply to the thirsty vineyards whose rocky soils have been depleted during the growing season. We wake each morning to a blanket of fog, the highest ridges of mountains on the horizon just poking through.

In the evenings, it's time to hunker down inside. Our fireplace rotisserie comes out of storage, and the smell of spit-roasting meat fills the house when it's called into duty. We roast chestnuts over the open flames, shell them, and squash them flat with the palms of our hands to intensify their flavor as our Tuscan friends have taught us to do. We think about the year that's just passed and wonder about the next to come . . .

Antipasto: Coccoli con prosciutto crudo (page 160)—*Deep-Fried Dough Balls with Prosciutto and Stracchino Cheese*

Primo: La ribollita (page 76)—*Tuscan Black Kale and Bean Soup*

Secondo: Brasato di manzo al chianti (page 143) con cime di rapa saltate (page 242)—*Slow-Braised Beef Shoulder in Chianti Wine with Sautéed Broccoli Rabe*

SOURCES

ONLINE AND MAIL ORDER

Eataly Extra-virgin olive oils, dried pasta, canned tomatoes, and double zero flour. www.eataly.com

Gustiamo Extra-virgin olive oils, vinegars, canned San Marzano tomatoes, dried pasta, anchovies, sea salt, capers, Parmigiano-Reggiano cheese, honey and miscellaneous pantry items. www.gustiamo.com

Olive Oil Jones Hand-selected extra-virgin olive oils and vinegars. www.oliveoiljones.com

Lobel's of New York Prime dry-aged beef, heritage pork, veal, and chicken. www.lobels.com

D'Artagnan Wild boar, duck, guinea hen, quail, and other game. www.dartagnan.com

La Cantinetta del Chianti Italian wines, olive oil, vinegars, honey, dried pasta, condiments, and jarred specialty foods. Shipping worldwide. www.lacantinettadelchianti.it

Enoteca Porciatti Italian wines, olive oil, honey, dried pasta, prepared sauces, and condiments. Shipping worldwide. www.casaporciatti.it

GUIDE TO LOCAL RESTAURANTS AND WINE BARS

IN CHIANTI

Lo Sfizio de' Bianchi (Gaiole-in-Chianti) Casual, traditional, family-style trattoria serving pizza, pastas, and local specialties. Well-curated wine list focused on local producers. House-baked pastries. Not to be missed: house-made tiramisu.

Osteria di Brolio (Castello di Brolio; Gaiole-in-Chianti) Upscale Tuscan dishes with a twist near the historic Castello di Brolio winery and Ricasoli family residence. Library selection of Brolio wines available by the glass or bottle.

I' Galletto 'Briaco (Gaiole-in-Chianti) Family-run trattoria serving homey, gutsy Chiantigiana-style dishes.

Taverna Le Cose Buone (Gaiole-in-Chianti) Chef/owner of Apulian roots preparing high-quality fish and seafood specialities, a rarity in Chianti.

La Gorgia Vino & Cucina (Gaiole-in-Chianti) Small but thoughtfully curated menu of creative dishes by husband/wife team in a warm and welcoming space. House specialty: risotto finished tableside in a wheel of Parmigiano-Reggiano.

Osteria Il Bandito (Gaiole-in-Chianti) Ten minutes from the town center. A simple osteria affording commanding views of the surrounding countryside. Grilled meats, pastas, and traditional side dish accompaniments. House specialty: Sardinian-style roast suckling pig available by preorder/reservation.

La Cantinetta del Chianti (Gaiole-in-Chianti) Carefully curated selection of local wines that can be enjoyed by the glass or bottle accompanied by small tapas-style plates of cured meats, cheeses, and other specialty items. Available Tuesdays: fresh buffalo mozzarella from Campania.

Trattoria Il Carlino d'Oro (Gaiole-in-Chianti; località San Regolo) One minute around the corner and up the hill from the Castello di Brolio winery, this small trattoria with sweeping views of the surrounding countryside serves simple, hearty, Chiantigiana-style fare. Wide selection of antipasti, soups, pastas, and grilled and roasted meats. Lunch only.

Ristorante Badia a Coltibuono (Gaiole-in-Chianti) Upscale restaurant at the historic monastery property that serves as the headquarters of the Badia a Coltibuono winery. Magnificent views of the surrounding countryside from the outdoor terrace in warm-weather months. Creative menu rooted in local ingredients and Tuscan tradition. Deep library selection of Coltibuono wines supplemented by a small but thoughtfully curated list of other notable local producers.

Ristorante La Taverna di Vagliagli (Vagliagli) Live-fire, open-hearth Tuscan cooking at its best. Grilled meats, chicken, and game. Ample selection of house-made pastas, soups, and risotto. Excellent selection of local wines.

La Taverna della Berardenga (Castelnuovo di Berardenga) Classic bottega/bar/trattoria on the edge of Castelnuovo's town center. Full range of traditional Tuscan antipasti, primi, and secondi. Specialties: pici cacio pepe, roast duck "in porchetta," and bistecca alla fiorentina.

Enoteca Porciatti (Radda-in-Chianti) Well-stocked selection of fine wines from throughout Italy (and France) with a focus on Chianti and Brunello di Montalcino. Full menu of antipasti, pastas, soups, and meat dishes all prepared with ingredients sourced from the family's adjacent bottega/butcher shop.

IN FLORENCE

Ristorante Buca dell'Orafo Off-the-beaten-path classic Florentine trattoria. Look for specialties that typically can't be found elsewhere: groppa scaloppata, la francesina, maltagliati al sugo con pecorino, and tortino ai funghi porcini.

Trattoria Camillo A Florence institution. White-tablecloth trattoria patronized by locals and tourists alike. Extensive menu including daily seasonal specials from the Florentine tradition. Exceptional service by vested waiters in black bow ties—many with more than twenty years of tenure.

Ristorante Buca Lapi A temple of grilled meats and house-made pastas in a casual but elegant setting. Just off the very chic (and very expensive) Via Tornabuoni shopping district.

Marina di Santo Spirito Fresh fish and pristine seafood in an eclectic and welcoming space in Florence's Oltrarno neighborhood. Live music on many evenings.

Pitti Gola e Cantina One of Florence's best enotecas. Young, knowledgeable, and passionate staff/owners focused on small artisanal wine producers from throughout Italy. Special emphasis on Tuscan wines. Personalized dinners and lunches with guided wine pairings available on reservation.

Trattoria Da Burde Old-school institution serving all the classics of the Florentine tradition in a fun, lively setting. Excellent wine list. Located well off the beaten path, but worth the ten-minute taxi ride from the historic center.

Da Delfina (Artimino) Forty minutes west of Florence in the hills of Carmignano lies the small medieval village of Artimino, well worth a visit itself for its charm and history. But Da Delfina is the real reason for the trip. A live-fire rotisserie produces mouthwatering specialities in the colder-weather months and a constantly rotating selection of house-made pastas makes choosing difficult. Well-curated wine list with a special emphasis on Carmignano, a small wine region often overlooked by international visitors.

GUIDE TO REGIONAL WINERIES

IN CHIANTI CLASSICO

Castello di Ama One of Chianti's best and most iconic wine producers. Tours and tastings available upon reservation. On-property restaurant serving both lunch and dinner. Added bonus: dozens of contemporary art installations throughout the property's ancient "borgo" by artists from around the world. Località Ama, Gaiole-in-Chianti; www.castellodiama.com

Castello di Brolio The birthplace of Chianti Classico. On-site tasting room, casual bar, and upscale restaurant. Tours of the Ricasoli family estate and castello available. Località Brolio, Gaiole-in-Chianti; www.ricasoli.com

Rocca di Montegrossi Marco Ricasoli Firidolfi, a member of the Brolio-Ricasoli wine family dynasty, is producing his own carefully crafted wines in nearby Monti. Winery tours and tastings available strictly by advance reservation. Località San Marcellino, Monti-in-Chianti, Gaiole-in-Chianti; www.roccadimontegrossi.it

La Casa di Bricciano The brainchild of South African transplant and winery builder Peter de Pentheny O'Kelly, this under-the-radar local gem is now in the hands of Peter's son Rory. Small production of Chianti Classico and Super Tuscan wines. Tours and tastings available by reservation. Località La Casa di Bricciano, Gaiole-in-Chianti; www.lacasadibricciano.it

Capannelle Boutique wine resort set high above Gaiole with breathtaking views of the surrounding countryside. Tours, tastings, and on-property meals available by reservation. Limited number of guest rooms. Località Capannelle, Gaiole-in-Chianti; web.capannelle.it

IN MONTALCINO

Podere Le Ripi Winemaker Sebastian Nasello is a winner of the prestigious Giulio Gambelli award and a force within Montalcino's collegial winemaker community. Organized visits, guided tastings, and meals available by reservation. Of particular interest: the winery's organic farm and the unique spherical architecture of the winemaking facility. Località Le Ripi, Montalcino; www.podereleripi.com

Cupano Wines made with finesse, elegance, and a touch of French winemaking know-how. The Cupano portfolio, now in the capable hands of young winemaker Andrea Polidoro, features stellar examples of barrique-aged Brunellos, not the norm in this regional bastion of tradition nor often done very well. Small private tours can be arranged upon reservation. Località Camigliano, Montalcino; www.cupano.it

Castiglion del Bosco Although built on a large-scale production model, this Montalcino icon produces powerful, balanced wines of impressive stature. The winery is well equipped and staffed to welcome visitors for tours and guided tastings. Località Castiglion del Bosco, Montalcino; wine.castigliondelbosco.com

REGIONAL ACCOMMODATIONS

5-STAR

Borgo San Felice Completely renovated and refurbished "borgo" near Castelnuovo Berardenga featuring luxurious rooms and suites. Michelin-star dining in a beautifully appointed formal restaurant as well as more casual options poolside and at the property's rustic trattoria. www.borgosanfelice.it

Rosewood at Castiglion del Bosco Recognized by many as Tuscany's top resort, every detail has been carefully designed. Customer service of the highest level, including a variety of formal and casual dining options. Access to the nearby CdB private golf club is possible upon reservation through hotel guest services. www.rosewoodhotels.com/en/castiglion-del-bosco

Portrait Firenze Unbeatable location in the heart of Florence's historic center a stone's throw from the Ponte Vecchio. Leonardo Ferragamo's vision for modern luxury and top-notch service brings in guests from around the world drawn to this boutique hotel's warmth and comfort. www.lungarnocollection.com/portrait-firenze

4-STAR

Castello di Spaltenna Gaiole-in-Chianti's finest hotel situated in a restored medieval monastery with spa, pool, and formal and casual dining. www.spaltenna.it

Capannelle Wine Resort Small, intimate boutique wine resort with pool and magnificent views of the Chianti countryside. On-property dining available upon advance reservation. web.capannelle.it

3-STAR

Cavarchino B&B Small and well-tended bed and breakfast run with passion and warmth by local husband/wife owners. www.cavarchino.it

INDEX

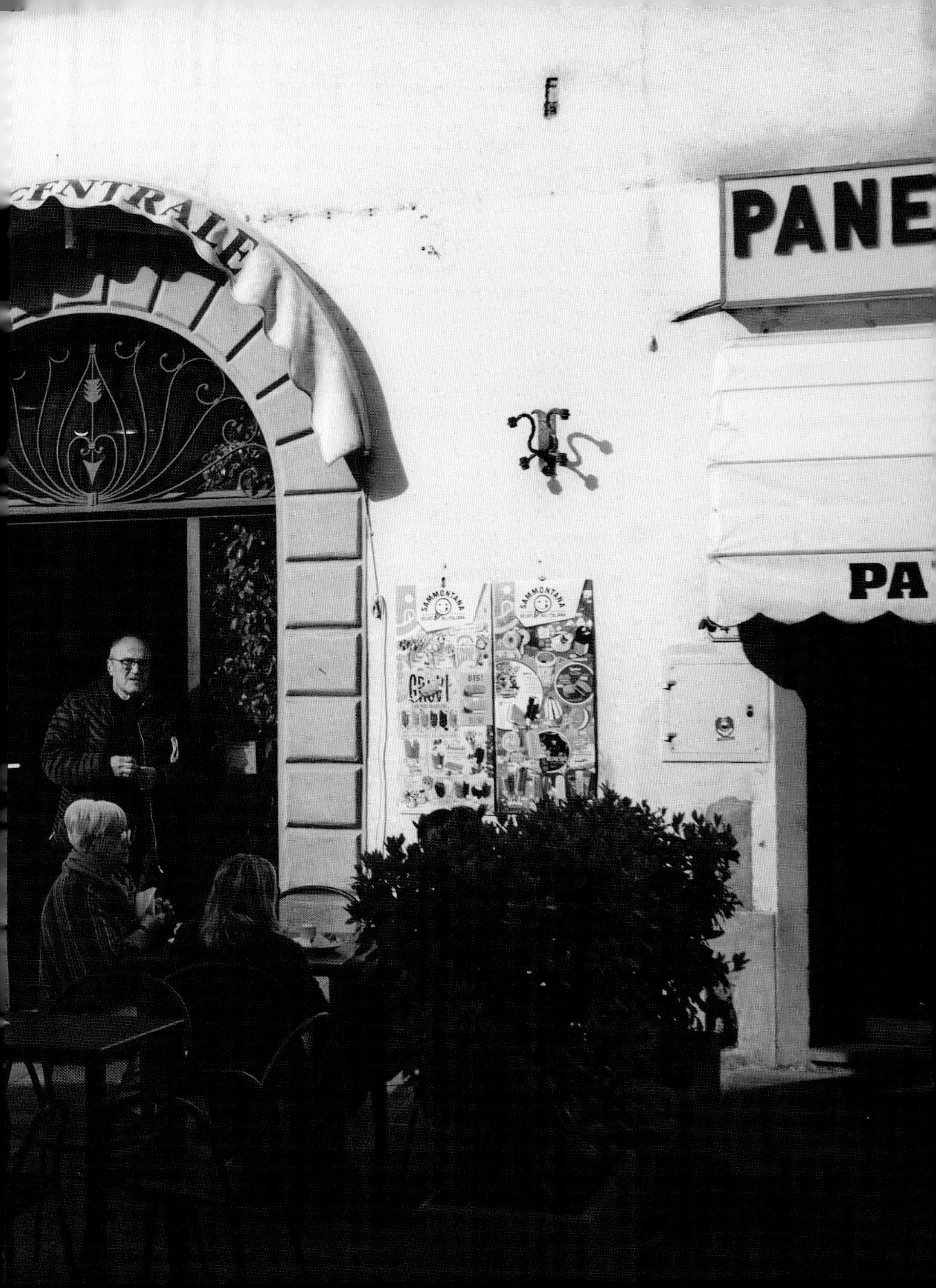
CENTRALE
PANE
PA
SAMMONTANA
SAMMONTANA
BIS!

ACKNOWLEDGMENTS

I've learned that making a cookbook is a lot like making wine. It takes a lot of hands with different perspectives, vision and talent. The text is like the grapes—the backbone of the endeavor. But then it's transformed into something more. Many people have touched this project with valued counsel, experience and shared passion.

First and foremost, to my "20 Amici." You are the inspiration for this book. I feel so lucky to include you all among my circle of friends. Vi voglio bene.

To Angela Engel and her team at The Collective Book Studio. Thank you for seeing the potential in this project and believing in me as a first-time author. Thank you to my editor, Amy Treadwell, for tirelessly and thoughtfully working with me through iteration after iteration, always with a keen eye toward bringing the stories and recipes to life on the page. Thank you, Rachel Lopez Metzger, for injecting another dimension to the book with your beautiful design.

If it's true that a finished dish's aesthetic is integral to its appeal, the same can be said of a cookbook. For this one in particular, where a sense of people and place is fundamental to understanding the food, I knew that the imagery would be of utmost importance. No one could have done a better job of transporting the reader into our town and our kitchen than Nico Schinco. Nico—you are a great talent and a wonderful collaborator. Thank you, not only for the beautiful images you captured, but for embracing the project on a very personal level and sharing my vision. Can't wait for our next "viaggio nel vortice. . . ."

A big thank you also to my incredible team in New York City. Katie Wayne—your skill in the kitchen, which is beyond awesome, may be surpassed only by your cool demeanor and organization. Thank you for working with me to bring these dishes to life. Maeve Sheridan—your sense of style, eye for detail and boundless energy shine throughout these pages. Thank you for coming to Gaiole. Next time I promise there will be an antiquarian fair on the itinerary.

I would have been lost without the help of my pre-production assistant in Italy (and Gaiolese DOCG), Gaia Cavaciocchi. Grazie di cuore cara. Sei fantastica.

Joe Barbieri . . . Who knew, when we randomly met thirty years ago, that a lifelong friendship was being forged? Your encouragement and advice throughout this project were invaluable. Thank you for being my trusted sounding board.

And finally, to my wife and best friend, Cyndy. Thank you for always being there; for always sharing my dreams as if they were your own; for always believing in me, even when tackling something—like writing this book—that seems farfetched. I love you infinity.

John Bersani, August 2024

ABOUT THE AUTHOR

John Bersani is a writer, teacher, and passionate advocate of Italian food, wine, and culture. A second-generation Italian American with roots in his grandparent's kitchen, John's cooking philosophy has been shaped by more than twenty years of living in a small hilltop town in central Tuscany. When he's not in the kitchen, chances are John is off sharing his inside knowledge of the Tuscan countryside with small bespoke tour groups, discovering new culinary inspiration up and down the Italian boot, or spending time with his wife and three adult children. This is his first cookbook. John is the founder of Avventura Trips (www.avventuratrips.com). He and his wife, Cyndy, split their time between Gaiole-in-Chianti, Italy, and Snowmass Village, Colorado.

ABOUT THE PHOTOGRAPHER

Nico Schinco is a photographer based in Queens NY. Working in food, cookbooks, travel, still-life, and editorial, his work shines when documenting the stories of people close and far, along with exceptional food, drink, and landscapes. His recent work can be seen in *Pasta Every Day* from Voracious and *Salty, Cheesy, Herby, Crispy Snackable Bakes* from Countryman Press.